THE TEACHINGS OF DON CARLOS

—THE— TEACHINGS —OF— DON CARLOS

PRACTICAL APPLICATIONS OF THE WORKS OF CARLOS CASTANEDA

VICTOR SANCHEZ

TRANSLATION BY
ROBERT NELSON

BEAR & COMPANY
PUBLISHING
SANTA FE, NEW MEXICO

LIBRARY OF CONGRESS CATALOGING-IN-PUBLICATION DATA

Sánchez, Victor,
    [Enseñanzas de don Carlos. English]
    The teachings of don Carlos : practical applications of the
works of Carlos Castaneda / Victor Sanchez ; translation by
Robert Nelson.
        p. cm.
    Includes bibliographical references and index.
    ISBN 1-879181-23-1
    1. Shamanism. 2. Castaneda, Carlos, 1931– . 3. Altered state
of consciousness. 4. Shamans—Mexico. I. Nelson, Robert.
II. Title.
BF1615.S2613 1995   94-48657
229'.7—dc20   CIP

Bear & Company, Inc.
Santa Fe, NM 87504-2860

Cover design: Lightbourne

Interior design: Marilyn Hager

Typography: Marilyn Hager

Printed in the United States by BookCrafters

1 3 5 7 9 8 6 4 2

SPECIAL NOTICE
TO THE READER

This book is a reference work and as such is intended solely for use as a source of general information and not for application to any individual case. The exercises in this book have been taught in workshops by the author; some of them involve the potential of physical risk, such as #73 (Alpinism Arboreal), and #75 (Burial of the Warrior), and they were intended to be experienced in groups conducted by experienced practitioners. Individuals need to be in adequate physical condition, as determined by a physician, to practice some of the more rigorous exercises, such as the ones detailed above. Any and all difficulties or injuries that occur in the practical application of this material are solely the responsibility of the individual, or are the responsibility of practitioners using such exercises in their group sessions.

CONTENTS

ACKNOWLEDGMENTS

I have had the privilege of knowing and receiving, perhaps undeservedly, the love of many people. And there are also many people to whom I would have to give thanks. If I were to list all of those who in one way or another have contributed or participated in the experiences that led to the publication of this work, there probably would not be enough pages in this book to include them all.

I wish, nevertheless, to publicly thank some of those beings who have had the greatest influence on this facet of my efforts:

To the mountains, the trees, and the gray whales who gave to me secrets of harmony and power while allowing me to know a type of communication beyond the agreements and disagreements in the world of humans.

To the indigenous peoples who accepted me into their world as a fellow human being.

To the woman who, besides giving me life, taught me the first song of love I ever knew, and whose melody continues to this day to beautify my world.

To the participants in the work groups, who made possible the generation of so much magic, which we all shared together.

To Tere, for all these years of love and growth.

To my father, for his intransigence during a lifetime of battling against mediocrity.

And, of course, to Carlos Castaneda, for pointing out to us a doorway and giving us the key through the publication of the most amazing books of our time.

Victor Sanchez

KEY TO BOOKS BY CARLOS CASTANEDA CITED IN TEXT

(I) *The Teachings of Don Juan*

(II) *A Separate Reality*

(III) *Journey to Ixtlan*

(IV) *Tales of Power*

(V) *The Second Ring of Power*

(VI) *The Eagle's Gift*

(VII) *The Fire From Within*

(VIII) *The Power of Silence*

INTRODUCTION

ABOUT THE AUTHOR

The book you hold in your hands is the result of my walking many steps over the Earth, driven by curiosity and the wish to live a life different from those I had observed since infancy, lives that seemed to reflect only the gray color of the unhappy repetitions of normal people. The curiosity brought me to witness unsuspected corners of our Earth, to merge myself with nature through joy and unusual efforts. It brought me to discard the old structure of my life through my encounters with the others, who were both indigenous Nahuas and Huicholes as well as the explorers of insanity; the participants in my encounter groups; those loyal dogs with whom I have shared much of my life; the great whales who allowed me to share their world; and my closest loved ones.

I look back and each step, each instant, brings me a feeling born in the heat of my search for freedom and for my unknown face.

My search took me first to the place of my origin; I trod many paths over this Mexican land that has sheltered and nurtured me in her bosom. As I walked over her soil, she received me, revealing to me many secrets. She brought me into contact with those who live closest to her: the indigenous peoples from the steep sierras of central Mexico, bearers of a knowledge that could rescue us from our perennial troubles, or rescue any one individual for that matter. Among the Nahuas of that remote solitude, I left behind my name and my history, letting go of who I once was, and was reborn in the din of my encounter with the "otherness".

As a man of my time, I decided to study anthropology, to equip myself with the necessary tools that would assist me in constructing a bridge between my native society and the magical world of the Indians. Working with anthropologists, I discovered they were too interested in transforming the Indians, teaching ethnocentric ideas such as progress, nationality, awareness of social class, to facilitate communication between them and us. These anthropologists are similar to the conquistadors during the sixteenth century in their lust for conquest and the clergy in their desire to convert the native populations to Christianity.

Disillusioned, I invented what I call anti-anthropology, following the example of those psychiatrists who invented anti-psychiatry to tear down the obstacles placed by traditional psychiatry for fear of encountering the *otherness* of people regarded as clinically insane. So I turned anthropology around, stood it on its head so to speak. I approached the *otherness* of the Indians, not to transform them but to transform myself; to encounter my unknown face by submerging myself in, what was to me, an alien view of reality. This reality preserves many of the ancient secrets of knowledge the Toltecs learned directly from the world.

Later—about 13 years ago—I stumbled on the works of Carlos Castaneda. It surprised me to find in them much of what I had experienced in my own fieldwork, only there was a degree of complexity and systematization I had not met with previously. The *dreaming body*, the way of the warrior, awareness of the Earth, the correct form of walking, access to nonordinary reality, omens, signs, the tonal and the nagual—all were themes I had encountered among different ethnic groups such as the Huicholes, Mazatecs, Mixtecs, and principally, the Nahuas. Besides finding a system for these ideas, I also found in "the teachings" many themes, suggestions, and proposals that I had not, until then, encountered. Most interesting of all was that there, spread throughout Castaneda's writings, was a large quantity of specific possibilities for action, which appealed to me a great deal.

THE CONVERTED ANTHROPOLOGIST
AND THE POLEMIC

For those readers who may not know, in the early 1960s Carlos Castaneda was an anthropology student about to graduate when he met an old Yaqui Indian named Juan Matus. With don Juan as his informant, Castaneda attempted to study the medicinal uses of peyote among the Indians of the southwestern United States and northern Mexico. The old Indian revealed himself as a powerful man of knowledge, a sorcerer, and he took Carlos as his apprentice from the beginning of their relationship. Little by little the young anthropologist grew into his role as don Juan's apprentice and in the eight books published to date[1], he has described the different stages of that apprenticeship—sparking a great deal of interest among readers worldwide.

Castaneda's works have generated much controversy, especially among anthropologists. Perhaps jealous of the success he has enjoyed, they were disposed to criticize, claiming that his writings have no basis in truth, particularly regarding the existence of don Juan as a real person. I personally have not had the pleasure of knowing don Juan, but I do know don Carlos and I have read and made use of his books. The question of whether don Juan existed or not seems to me insignificant in comparison with the ideas set forth in these books. Personally, I am not particularly interested if the ideas came from don Juan or from Castaneda. The fact is they exist and—most important—they work. Putting these teachings into practice reveals that in each one of us there lies hidden another awareness—the awareness of the other self—which opens unlimited possibilities of perception and experience. This is what is really significant.

Therefore, throughout the ensuing pages, I will refer to Carlos Castaneda and to don Juan interchangeably as the creators or bearers of a complex system of knowledge. That is

---

[1] 1991—see bibliography of Carlos Castaneda books, p.229.

how they present themselves to us: together, in the same work, the binomial Castaneda/don Juan inviting us to penetrate into their mysterious world. Thus, I abstain from commenting on something that is totally out of my reach— namely, to affirm or deny the existence of someone whom I've never seen, a matter that seems irrelevant.

THE READERS

Perhaps what attracted me to Castaneda's works from the beginning were the poetic feelings they provoked. The perennial search for freedom and the mystery that surrounds the world of the warrior express the secret feelings of all humanity. But all poetry and proposals of freedom aside, it would appear that the majority of the readers of his works have not known how to make use of their contents.

Among his readers are commonly found those who consider his books as amusing literary fiction, regarding them as nothing more than entertainment. The obsessive intellectual will usually discard them as simple fiction, and rate them worthless as to literary value. And for not so mysterious reasons, there are those fanatic intellectuals who seem to feel bothered by the writings of Castaneda and above all by the irreverent don Juan, who was always so ready to make a mockery of intellectual pursuits. Could this be why they tend to reject Castaneda's writings? Perhaps. At any rate, it is true that intellectual types in general do not read Castaneda (although there are a good many, especially in academic circles, who read him covertly).

On the other end of the scale we have the fanatic, who without any concrete experience regarding these teachings, takes everything as the truth, trying to understand it literally. This is the kind of person who goes around "seeing" allies and power places at every turn. All of this is, of course, a product of the imagination rather than experience. They are fanatics not because they like the works of Carlos Castaneda, but rather for not being able or not wanting to take the trouble to put into practice the proposals put forth in the writings—which requires unbending purpose. They instead supply their imagination with fantasies in place of what their lazy existence will not permit them to experience directly.

Near to the fanatic are those aficionados of marihuana and other drugs, who use the writings of Castaneda to justify their addictions. They believe that, through the leisurely consumption of a stupefacient, they will acquire "seriousness" by the mere fact of disguising their habit as a "search for knowledge". Like the fanatic, the drug addict substitutes fantasies and verbal discussions for concrete work, with the added difficulty that those fantasies become more vivid, thanks to the influence of the drugs. The drugs, of course, without any change in routines, can alter nothing in his or her ego or daily life.

Even when the drug addict has access to "power plants" such as those used in indigenous rituals, he or she manages to turn the use of these magic plants (peyote, toloache, mushrooms, etc.) into something that resembles mere drunkenness. They reinforce structural limitations, signifying an escape from reality rather than an encounter with it. Naturally, it is another thing entirely among indigenous peoples who use the power plants to aid the process of knowledge inherited from their ancestors, and which they follow with strict discipline and preparation. The two situations have nothing in common.

There also are readers belonging to neither of the aforementioned mentioned groups who find the ideas attractive but simply do not know how to carry out the proposals contained therein.

Thus, in spite of the value of Castaneda's writings and their popularity, they have not been made use of adequately. In fact, the majority of his readers fall into one of these three categories.

Careless reading of these books, coupled with the deep-rooted absentmindedness of modern peoples, keeps the real treasure of don Juan's teaching inaccessible to almost every-one. Therefore, I have given myself the task of suggesting a method by which to approach the mysterious world revealed to us by Carlos Castaneda.

A LIVING STUDY OF HIS WORK

It is not necessary to either condemn a priori the works of Castaneda or to dogmatically accept them as an ideological doctrine. There exists an exact way to approach them: through a living study of the techniques and exercises con-tained therein. I have worked precisely in this way for the last eleven years, and have made the discovery that there are complete areas of our being and of our feeling that we have forgotten due to our cultural conditioning. These can, however, be recovered. There exist both another reality and another way of living. And it is worth the trouble to work in order to experience them.

GROUP WORK

I decided early on to practice by myself. I combined my excursions to the country with many of the techniques pro-posed by Castaneda. My findings were so earthshaking that I set myself the task of communicating them to others, to share them and to find out if these techniques worked as well for other people. Thus were born my first work groups eleven years ago.

Although years later I had the pleasure of knowing Carlos personally—in whose person I observed an extraordi-nary congruence with what he had written—my work has developed independently. In fact, I believe that Castaneda's work was written specifically to motivate us to apply these ideas in a practical manner. This book deals primarily with the form in which I have responded to that motivation and the results thus obtained.

In my work groups, I developed methods of self-learning through group participation. These were first labeled "The

Other Sorcery," alluding to ignored aspects of sorcery, then later "The Art of Living Purposefully," putting emphasis on the search for ways of being and living that expressed the freedom of the warrior. In workshops in the field, we took on the task of reinventing ourselves and rescuing our awareness of the other self. Techniques developed from Castaneda's works were put into practice as well as those born of my own experience with the Indians; these were complemented with techniques generated by the group activity itself. Our work always dealt with practical applications, not with intellectual discussions.

In this work I never considered myself a master—since there are no masters who can live our lives for us or walk in our footsteps—but as just one more participant, interested in continually developing the same knowledge he was proposing to everyone else. My particular role was to coordinate—drawing on my experience—the work of everyone concerned, including my own.

THE ULTIMATE NOT-DOING

Motivated by the results of our group work, some years ago I conceived the idea of writing a book about the teachings of don Carlos and the practical way we had approached them. However with the life I had chosen to lead, I found myself constantly traveling. Each trip to the country, each new group formed, demanded my total participation. There was no time for something that seemed so cold as to sit in front of a computer screen and write.

On the other hand, for a man of my nature, always inclined toward action—climbing mountains, hiking through jungles and deserts, diving in the ocean, or exploring caves—to sit still for hours and write represented the ultimate not-doing that would demand that I go beyond my limits. Since I was not a writer, I had to create one using myself as the raw material.

Finally the moment arrived. Life took hold of me and I

knew it would not let go until I had completed the task. I suspended my work with the groups and disappeared for a time to take on the challenge of converting myself into a writer— although only for as long as it took to write this book.

THE BOOK

The title, *The Teachings of Don Carlos*, was chosen to attract the attention of those who have been fascinated by the world and the mysteries revealed through the works of Castaneda, but who have not found occasion or method by which they might bring to their lives some of the magic that characterizes the solitary realm of the nagual. This title alludes to the peculiar relationship of apprentice to teacher that we—in a manner of speaking—establish with the author each time we enrich our world through the practice of some of the proposals contained in his books.

MOTIVATION AND CONTRIBUTIONS

One motivation for writing was that the majority of Castaneda's readers, while fascinated by the content of his writings, seemed to be confused by them as regards their possibilities of concrete application, and above all by the strange realities and facets of the world they describe. Works by other authors on the subject of Castaneda were not much help. And there was much criticism and gossip, FBI-style, about the "Castaneda enigma." In no way did these critics touch upon his substantial proposals simply because they did not understand or had glossed over the writings of don Carlos, merely repeating awkwardly what he had already so masterfully described.

Someone was needed to show how to carry out Castaneda's proposals within the context of the life of *homo urbanus*. Many have said: "I imagine. I suppose. I understand. I have compared, analyzed, or thought about the teachings" or some such thing. Very few have said: "I have done. I have put into practice. I have experienced. I have lived." What was lacking was a book about practical application, not speculation.

This is why I felt I had something to say. I chose, from the totality of my work, the material that relates to my personal as well as group experience and to the assimilation through direct living experience, of *The Teachings of Don Carlos*. While the quality of this work is not mine to judge, I will say I put my heart into the task. If by this simple proposal, I contribute something that can be carried into the everyday world, making it more gratifying, or complete, or at least more fun, I will be satisfied.

THE PERIPHERAL CONNECTION TO "THE RULE"

Readers in general do not know don Juan or even don Carlos, but they have found in Castaneda's work a door left slightly ajar. If they open it by the force of their own efforts, they will connect themselves with the tradition of which his works speak, although in an unorthodox fashion—namely, taking his writings as a point of reference for action. This eventually will result in (in fact it is already happening) a large number of more or less solitary warriors, connected peripherally with the party of the nagual. (Perhaps the mysterious "three pronged nagual" [VI-232][2] mentioned in *The Eagle's Gift*, refers to this happening.)

Independent of this, however, the possibilities proposed in work such as Castaneda's are of concern to everyone because they relate to unexplored facets of awareness that are present in every one of us.

---

[2] To make it easier to locate those passages in the work of Castaneda that relate to my exposition, I have included a simple system of reference: a Roman numeral signifies each of his books according to the order in which they were published, after which appears the page number in arabic numerals (eg., III-201). See "Key to Carlos Castaneda Books Cited in Text" on p. x, or "Bibliography of Carlos Castaneda Books", p. 229.

FREEDOM AND KNOWLEDGE
AS PERSONAL RESPONSIBILITY

One of the fundamental proposals of my work is that we each can give ourselves the task of rescuing our unknown possibilities of awareness without the specific presence of someone else to help us achieve it. In our own beings there already exist the tools necessary. When we are ready to give up being "warriors of the sofa", to convert ourselves into committed practitioners, the slightest opportunity from outside will be enough to send us on our way. This will come sooner or later in the form of a sorcerer, a book, a work group, or anything else providing the needed impetus, but ultimately, what counts are the individual efforts each person is willing to make.

I think what was said about the rescue of our unknown possibilities can be applied to the search for freedom as well. Freedom, however, cannot come from outside since in reality it is strictly a personal responsibility. I speak of a freedom that we can conceive or intuit—without necessarily understanding it—within the context of our own life. A liberal or fantasy vision of freedom has the disadvantage of being so perfect and extraneous that we would have no way of approaching it; therefore we remain passive in the face of the limitations of our everyday existence. I am proposing an approximation on a practical, rather than mental, level of freedom and knowledge. For me, the knowledge displayed by any human being expresses itself in his or her way of living, not in words.

WORKING WITHOUT A TEACHER

✓   In *The Power of Silence*, don Juan explains that we can follow the path of knowledge and the "return to the spirit" (VII-180) by our own efforts, carrying out simple actions to save the necessary energy to move the assemblage point. (The terms "movement of the assemblage point" and "saving energy" as well as their practical application will be explained throughout this work.) Don Juan put it this way:

> "Our difficulty with this simple progression . . . is
> that most of us are unwilling to accept that we need so
> little to get on with. We are geared to expect instruction,
> teaching, guides, masters. And when we are told that
> we need no one, we don't believe it. We become ner-
> vous, then distrustful, and finally angry and disappoint-
> ed. If we need help, it is not in methods, but in
> emphasis. If someone makes us aware that we need to
> curtail our self-importance, that help is real. Sorcerers
> say we should need no one to convince us that the
> world is infinitely more complex than our wildest fan-
> tasies. So, why are we dependent? Why do we crave
> someone to guide us when we can do it ourselves? . . ."
> (VIII-180).

In things having to do with knowledge, we are inundated
with masters and disciples. But there are no masters. There
are no disciples. There are people who are going to die, the
difference being that some realize it and others don't. Real
knowledge that affects the way we live and the way we die
cannot be transmitted; only by means of personal experience
is it acquired. Books, masters, schools, and gurus are useful
aids only when we are ready to perform concrete acts in the
inexhaustible task of knowledge.

It is very easy—which explains its popularity—to fall
under the spell of a master or "guru" possessor of knowledge
and power from whom, thanks to his goodness, we can
receive "illumination". The "sublime master" touches us with
a finger, "illuminating" us and waking our inner "shakti".
These illusions serve (especially in the West) to satisfy the
artificial needs of enraptured beings too weak to conceive of
the possibility of escaping from their miserable situation by
the force of their own efforts. Always there is someone else
who will save us, who will guide us. As children it was
mother and father; as adults it is the husband, the wife, the
sensei, or the "beloved guru".

In one way or another, self-deprecation takes control: "I am too weak. I can't do it alone. I need someone to guide me." And of course, we are oversupplied with "masters," "gurus," "schools," "esoteric sects," and others ready to take advantage, converting into hard cash that desire to be dominated that frequently takes hold of so many people.

A warrior is called that because he or she is always at war. Mommy is not needed to tell warriors what or what not to do. Warriors take responsibility as the guide in their lives and they are the force that moves them down their path toward knowledge, sure of their steps and their actions. As don Juan said: ". . . a warrior is impeccable when he trusts his personal power, regardless of whether it is small or enormous . . ." (III-183).

If a person is responsible, the books, schools, or masters can then serve as useful aids, their suggestions can be used as guides for action. However, it will be the solid terrain of facts that will determine whether such suggestions are personally useful or not.

In my work with groups, I don't ask that people believe in my words. There has been too much of that. We've believed too much, until we die without having known that life was spent waging battles that were not ours to begin with. Instead of belief, we need action. What I believe is not important. What matters is what I can do, live, create—everything having to do with the concrete, not with fantasy.

THE INDEXES OF KNOWLEDGE

The books of Carlos Castaneda, which to me have been so very useful—and this work that I hope will be useful to someone else—do not contain knowledge. They refer to knowledge but they are not the knowledge itself. As Castaneda himself told me on one occasion: ". . . in those 'damn books' (referring to his own works) one will not find knowledge; they are merely indexes. You yourself must be capable of putting into practice the proposals contained ✓ therein in order to understand what these indexes indicate. You have to walk on your own two feet, in the direction they point, to corroborate for yourself and to experience the knowledge to which they refer".[3] This still seems to me to be a very appropriate way to utilize books, masters, and schools, especially if these masters, books, and schools are sincere. In the same way, I suggest to interested readers: don't believe or disbelieve what I say in this book; try putting into practice its proposals, which is the only authentic way to know the freedom, power, and knowledge to which I so often refer.

REALITIES AND TALES OF POWER

The material in this book does not attempt to embrace the entire content of Castaneda's writings for the simple reason that many parts of his work remain mysterious to me. My purpose here is not to discuss what I have imagined or what others have told me. Rather I have related only that which I have lived through my own experience. Except for the first chapter, which presents a summary of the donjuanist vision of reality, the bulk of this book deals with techniques I have practiced and whose results I have corroborated.

I neither affirm nor deny those parts of his work that remain mysterious me, because I believe the affirmation or negation of the unknown equally erroneous and presumptuous. The way to deal with the mysterious is suggested to us by don Juan himself when he speaks of "tales of power" (IV-62). The majority of the themes touched upon in this work were for me, in the beginning, nothing more than tales of power; they simply made me curious. Working with them and experiencing them has converted them into realities of power for me. It was not a matter of belief but one of acting and corroborating. This method I recommend for anyone interested in similar mysteries: neither believe nor deny anything, but let these incredible tales of power remain thus

---

[3] Meeting with Carlos Castaneda, Mexico City, 1984.

until, through experience, they become a reality.

In the same way I do not claim that my way of approaching and understanding Castaneda's ideas is the ultimate truth, reflecting unequivocally his meaning in every instance. The present volume is nothing more than a testimony to the particular way in which I approached the experience, what I found, and how I used it. With my results I do not attempt to establish a unique truth, although I think they are consistent enough to make them worth the reader's trouble.

THE STRUCTURE OF THE BOOK

First I reemphasize that this is a work of practical consultation. Its principle part is composed of techniques for the concrete practice of each one of the themes that make it up. The major part of the exercises described are my own, using as a starting point the more or less general techniques or proposals from the work of Castaneda.

I have tried not to repeat those exercises that are explained in the original work, except those that lack sufficient detail to be carried out practically. There is no point in repeating words when the reader can consult Castaneda's work directly. Nevertheless, to facilitate consulting and locating the techniques in such a case, in the appendix there is a glossary classification of techniques, including the page number where they can be found in each book.

In general I have avoided reproducing work material that did not contain some novel contribution. Exceptions are the more detailed explanations of exercises that were imprecise in the original work and the variations or adaptations of these exercises to permit their execution in a context distinct from the original work and closer to that of the average reader. In many cases the exercises originated from techniques that I learned among the Indians or are free adaptations that may appear to have little to do with those found in the works of Castaneda. The latter were included—in spite of differences in external form—because they contain the same sustaining principles of donjuanist thinking and tend to produce similar results. All the exercises have as their general aim to make possible the movement of the assemblage point.

The book consists of ten chapters divided into three parts. The first and shortest constitutes a sort of organized summary of the basic concepts of the cosmovision of the warriors of the nagual's party, explaining the origin of the distinctive practices reviewed in part two and part three. The second and third parts comprise the practices for the right and left sides respectively. Such a division echoes the pedagogical system of don Juan, who divides his teachings in this manner, as will be detailed later on.

At the end are found a bibliography of Castaneda books, an annotated table of contents, and two glossaries. The first glossary contains nearly all of the techniques included in the eight books published to date (1991). The second lists all the exercises contained in the present work.

A SPHERICAL SYSTEM

Since the donjuanist system is absolutely not linear, but ✓ rather spherical, all of its parts are interrelated and each one leads to all the rest. It is not possible to define with precision an exact order in which to practice the techniques. As you will see, in many cases it is difficult to establish an exact dividing line between the different themes and exercises; one exercise will often involve aspects classified in different sections. For example, a walk of attention is properly an exercise of attention, but it also serves to stop the internal dialogue, has to do with corporal awareness, and so forth.

Therefore, this book can be read in any order, or the reader can go directly to the topic of interest without having read the preceding chapters. I do, however, recommend reading the entire work in order, since it is arranged in a certain way that will help a little to facilitate the process of self-learning.

As this is a work of practical consultation, it is evident that a simple reading of it—without carrying out the exercises—will not be sufficient for assimilating the knowledge it proposes. Due to the density of the material, I suggest that each chapter be read without haste, giving time to digest the contents of one before going on to the next.

I tend to use without distinguishing among them certain words such as sorcerer, person of knowledge, seer, warrior, in a way that might be expressed as: "people like don Juan or the warriors of his group." The specific use of each one is more a question of context and emphasis rather than a variation in meaning. In a similar vein, my use of the term "Western" refers to the common persons of today's industrial societies. I also call them modern, everyday, average, today's, and so forth.

And finally, my frequent use of the word "we," referring to things that I do or did with others, relates to the dynamics of interrelation within which occurred the major part of the experiences that form the foundation of this book. The efforts of many people have come together, whether deliberately or not, in attaining each one of the steps that have brought me to this point. Therefore this "we" should include the indigenous peoples who helped me to change amidst the lost mountains of the sierra; the people who have worked with me in groups, participants as well as coordinators; those dear beings who have accompanied me and enriched my life with the gift of their presence; and all those who eventually will come together in the collective and fraternal task of coloring with a little bit of magic a world made gray due to the neglect of our nature as luminous beings.

This "we" surely includes you, too, does it not?

Victor Sánchez

Miacatlan, Morelos
December 1991

— THE —
TEACHINGS
— OF —
DON CARLOS

PART ONE

REALITY ACCORDING TO DON JUAN

ONE

THE EAGLE'S EMANATIONS: A UNIVERSE OF ENERGY FIELDS

PRELIMINARIES

Although this book aspires to be of an eminently practical nature, in this first part I want to broadly outline the vision of reality that forms the basis of the complex system of knowledge and action of the warriors and seers of the nagual's party. Keep in mind that it represents only what we as external observers might call "the basic theories" of the doings of the sorcerer. For don Juan and his warriors none of this is theory, because they *see* and *live* the world in this way, while for an external observer such a world can only be imagined.

This is important because the practice of the exercises and techniques described herein constitutes, in my own experience, a doorway into the living experience of this separate reality. Precisely from the moment we become witnesses and participants in the experience of this *otherness* (relative to the separate reality of the self or the world) we penetrate into the alternate possibilities of our own perception and awareness. At that time the explanations of don Juan take on their true meaning, becoming useful tools for the understanding of realities that otherwise would submerge us in confusion.

The description of the world according to the tradition of don Juan furnishes us with a "road map" that allows us to understand and interact functionally with the reality lying beyond ordinary perception. In the same way, our ordinary description of reality, learned since infancy, aids us in understanding our experiences and interactions in the everyday world.

From this we can surmise that to function soberly and efficiently, whoever penetrates into a new world requires a view of that world distinct from the ordinary and congruent with its new living possibilities. This is precisely why, at the same time that he involves his apprentice in the execution of various pragmatic exercises, don Juan also provides him with numerous explanations of how the warriors of his party understand reality. And this is necessary for anyone who becomes involved in the way of the warrior by putting into practice the possibilities, both implicit and explicit, of the work of Castaneda. I refer to those who are seriously interested in experiencing the magic—beyond the pages of a book—within the realm of their own lives.

It should be mentioned that the ideas that follow do not in any way constitute a total panorama of "donjuanist thinking." They do emphasize those parts that directly relate to the areas where our work groups have made inroads, and it is precisely those to which I refer throughout this book. I will not dwell upon them at any great length, as it would require another work dedicated to this one objective alone to approach them in any great detail. Nevertheless, many of the themes I touch upon here will be developed in later chapters, together with their forms of concrete application.

THE ORIGIN

The origin of the vision of the world of don Juan Matus is rooted in the mysterious, although it is evident that it contains a multiethnic substratum and shares many of its significant elements with the indigenous world of Mesoamerica, particularly the Toltec universe. Such correlation can be found readily in the ethnohistorical information of pre-Colombian Mesoamerica, as well as through direct contact with the descendants of the Toltec culture currently alive—for example the Nahuas, Huicholes, and Maya. Concepts such as *tonal* and *nagual, the other self, the dreamed, the Earth as a conscious being,* are still used and practiced by the indigenous peoples of our time, almost at the dawn of the year 2000, as I have personally witnessed through my contacts with Indians of Toltec descent.

As for ourselves, the idea of a reality made up of fields of energy (which are not complete as we ordinarily perceive them) has been intuited continually down through the ages by the rest of humanity via such phenomena as religious visions, oriental philosophies of yoga and hinduism, modern theories of physics, and currents of modern thought such as phenomenology.[4]

In any case, it seems that no one has expressed a similar vision of reality with as much clarity and pragmatism as Carlos Castaneda does throughout his works. He emphasizes that the relativity of perception and the consequent existence of alternate realities are not mere philosophical speculation or an idle intellectual exercise. There are, in fact, genuine concrete applications on the level of perception and living experience of the individual, as we can readily observe in the extraordinary events that take place between the warriors of the nagual's party throughout the eight books mentioned.

---

[4] See Alfred Schutz, *The Phenomenology of the Social World,* Northwestern University Press, New York, 1984.

THE EAGLE'S EMANATIONS

For don Juan Matus, the existing world is not composed of objects as we see them but is made up of fields of energy that he terms "the eagle's emanations" (VI-283, in Spanish language editions only). These fields compose, in fact, the only transcendental reality. These emanations are grouped into great clusters or "bands" (VII-176), each making up an independent world. Don Juan speaks of the existence of forty-eight great bands of emanations, two of which are accessible to humans through our ordinary perception. One of these is the band of organic life; the second is a band that includes structures without consciousness—presumably minerals, gases, liquids, and so forth.

Inside the band of emanations of organic beings exists a strip relating in particular to the band of humanity which determines the narrow limits of the perception of the known. As each person does not align all the emanations in this band, there exist small variations in the possibilities of perception from person to person. These would include such cases as special sensitivity, extrasensory perception, psychic phenomena, or genius, or conversely, mental retardation, stupidity, or insensitivity.

The emanations normally aligned are known as normal awareness, the *tonal*, the right side. Inside the band of humanity are a large number of unused but accessible emanations that remain latent—though generally ignored—possibilities throughout a person's life. These constitute the anteroom of the unknown.

The emanations lying beyond the band of humanity constitute the unknown proper and as such are never aligned in the context of ordinary life. They are known as the *nagual*, a separate reality, the left side. Part of the work of don Juan and his group of warriors was devoted to developing the ability to align and perceive these emanations.

THE ASSEMBLAGE POINT

The factor that determines which emanations will be
selected or "aligned" (VII-66) in a given moment of perception is called the assemblage point (VII-126); it can be regarded as the property of awareness that selects the appropriate
emanations to produce the simultaneous perception of all the
elements that constitute the particular world being perceived.
The alignment of the assemblage point with certain bands of
emanations in particular, and specific emanations inside the
aligned band, is known as "the position of the assemblage
point". What this means for the average person is that his or
her assemblage point produces a singular alignment, which
is perceived as the everyday world.

A small movement in the position of the assemblage
point will produce an alignment of emanations normally dis-
regarded within the band of humanity. A large change will
align the assemblage point with the other great bands of
emanations.

The ultimate goal of this system of knowledge as set forth
by Castaneda is to achieve the deliberate movement of the
assemblage point to free the self from the confines of ordinary perception. Although moving the assemblage point is
not an easy task, in reality even small movements are enough
to produce enormous changes in any life, in the form of being
as well as in behavior and perception of the world.

The entire system of don Juan's teaching is geared toward
this goal. It is divided into two areas: the teachings for the
right side and the teachings for the left side. Each signifies in
its own way the forms of not-doing that enable the assemblage point to move, which are known as *stalking* and *dreaming* respectively.

The ability to perceive emanations is a faculty of living
beings that they continue to cultivate during their lives, causing perception to take place in specific ways. To cultivate per-

ception, each human is compelled—beginning at birth—to develop the capacity to select only a portion of the total emanations accessible to humans and to perceive them so that they function for that individual. If this were not done, the emanations would be perceived as incommensurable chaos.

THE FORMS OF ATTENTION

As has been mentioned, the factor of awareness determining the totality of the emanations perceived is called the assemblage point. The process of "skimming" (VI-284, in Spanish language editions only) the aligned emanations, grouping the appropriate ones while disregarding those deemed unnecessary (thus instilling order and meaning to the perception of objects), is called "attention" (VI-284, in Spanish language editions only) and is obtained from raw awareness by means of cultivating perception.

In agreement with the field in which it operates, attention is classified into three types, which are realized on three distinct levels: the first attention is the ordering of the perception in the world of the known; the second attention operates and puts order in the sphere of the unknown; and the third integrates the first two, allowing access to the unknowable.[5]

For ordinary people and for warriors in the initial phase of their apprenticeship, the first attention is the more important because it is the field of operation in which their lives take place. In fact, it is the specialized and strategic handling of his or her actions in the first attention that allows the warrior eventual access to the second.

The precise way in which the first attention selects and organizes the perceived emanations does not happen by chance; rather it responds to a specific training that is cultivated throughout our lives and whose fundamental features were rooted during the first years of our existence.

---

[5] As regards the third attention, I present it here the way Castaneda does in his work, although I hasten to point out that my experiences and practice to date remain restricted to the realm of the first and second attention, therefore, I can only consider it a "tale of power".

THE UNKNOWN AND THE UNKNOWABLE

Not all the emanations of the eagle are accessible to us; the vast majority of them occur in the realm of "the unknowable" (VII-60). In *The Fire From Within* don Juan affirms that the sphere of what can be known is made up of seven great bands of emanations (VII-182) that can—ultimately—become accessible to perception and that are divided into the known and the unknown.

The confines of the known are in reality a minuscule part of the total emanations available to us; nevertheless, they are the confines in which we, as ordinary people, remain for our entire lives, and they contain all the elements we perceive as reality in the everyday world. Everything that each person is and does lies within this part.

The unknown is a practically infinite part that for ordinary humans remains unexplored during the whole of life, although they have the possibility to reconnect themselves and perceive any part of the eagle's emanations included in it.

THE DESCRIPTION OF THE WORLD

At the moment of birth, babies do not perceive the world in the same way as do adults. Their attention is not yet functioning as the first attention, therefore they do not share the same perceptual world of those around them. Although surrounded by the same emanations, they have not yet learned to select and organize them as would an adult. This they will have to achieve, little by little, as they grow and assimilate the description of the world provided by their elders. Anyone, especially an adult, who comes into contact with a infant, in effect becomes a teacher—in most cases unconsciously—who incessantly describes the world to the child. Although children initially do not comprehend the description, eventually they will finally learn to perceive reality in terms of the description. It will be the description that determines the precise form in which their perception selects and organizes the fields of energy that surround them.

It is valid to say that what we perceive daily is the same description flowing constantly from ourselves toward the outside world. The flow of the description is generally constant, sustaining our familiar perception of the world, moment by moment, day after day. If the flow is suspended, our perception of the world collapses, resulting in what is known in the writings of Castaneda as "stopping the world" (III-13). *Seeing* refers to the capacity to perceive the world as it appears once the flow of the description has been interrupted (III-13).

During the initial phase of his apprenticeship with don Juan, Carlos is taught the description of the world according to sorcerers as a means of interrupting the flow of his ordinary description. Later he learns that it too is but a description in which he could become trapped (IV-240). Don Juan on more than one occasion declares that he is not a sorcerer but rather a warrior and seer.

THE INTERNAL DIALOGUE

The internal dialogue is the mental conversation that we sustain constantly with ourselves and is the most immediate expression of reality assimilated by everyone. Its function is that of a guardian whose fundamental task is to protect said description, nourishing it with its own contents (thoughts) and generating the doings that reinforce it. This implies that because of the things we talk to ourselves about, we perceive the world and behave as we do, which in turn tends to confirm the content and description of the internal dialogue. This can come to such extremes that we accustom ourselves to substitute thoughts in place of reality. We look at the world, the things, the people, or ourselves, at the same time thinking about what we see, and finish by taking our thoughts for the real thing. We tell ourselves the world is such and so and leave convinced that it is indeed thus.

Naturally, all of that which happens as a consequence of the internal dialogue ceases the moment we are able to stop said dialogue. This is why don Juan speaks of stopping the internal dialogue as the key that opens the door between the worlds (IV-233).

THE RINGS OF POWER

The ability to "skim" certain aligned emanations to agree ✓ with the terms of the description shared by the rest of humanity is called "the first ring of power", which we some- ✓ how attach to the elements of the world, projecting onto them our description of it. The result is our perception of the world such as we experience it. In addition, everyone's ring of power is attached to everyone else's, so the construction of reality in terms of the description is to a certain extent a collective task in which all those involved in a given specific situation participate. This makes the perception of each object more or less the same for everyone.

At the same time, there exists a second ring of power that ✓ allows perception to occur outside the ordinary description; this the sorcerer uses to construct other worlds (III-225). Although everyone has this second ring, it functions only when the first ring is shut down, a thing that rarely occurs in the life of ordinary people.

NOT-DOING

One way in which the first ring can be blocked is by performing actions foreign to our ordinary description of the world—what is known as *not-doing*. The ordinary description of the world compels us to behave always according to the terms it indicates; therefore, all actions emanate from said description and subsequently tend to revalidate it. These actions are what is known as "doing", and in combination with the description that nourishes them, they make up a system that is virtually self-sustaining. Any action that is not congruent with the description of the world would constitute a form of not-doing.

Not-doing interrupts the flow of the description, and this interruption in turn suspends the doing of the world of the known. Not-doing is the medium that opens the way to the unknown side of reality and of oneself. In other words, it provides access to the *nagual*—what is referred to in the case of the world as the *separate reality*, or in the case of an individual as the *awareness of the other self*.

Since not-doing practiced from right-side awareness has the power to bring us to facets of left-side awareness, its systematic practice creates points of contact between both sides. Little by little, this can bring us closer to the integration of both modes of awareness, resulting in what is known as "the totality of oneself".

THE EGO AS PART OF THE DESCRIPTION

Another aspect to be considered is that all we refer to when we say "I" (the ego) is also an element of the description we assimilate. This is especially significant if we realize that this part of the description keeps us chained to a form of being and behavior that—while it may appear absolute and definitive—can be interrupted or suspended entirely, opening unlimited possibilities in what we can be or do. In that sense, the not-doing that suspends the flow of the description represents an open door to freedom and change.

When by means of the not-doings of the personal self, we interrupt the flow of the description of our own person, we free ourselves from the enchantment of the ego—which wants us to believe that it represents the only reality. We can recognize then our true nature as fields of energy, free and fluid. Starting from that moment, we can take on the task of reinventing ourselves in an intentional and voluntary fashion, able to respond in novel ways to new situations that each moment provides for us.

THE TONAL AND THE NAGUAL

One of the more all-encompassing aspects of the don-juanist vision is the dual conception of reality expressed by the terms "tonal" and "nagual", without a doubt one of the many examples indicative of its pre-Columbian substratum. It is not difficult to establish the close relation between such concepts and the two facets of Ometeotl, the principal maintainer of the world in the ancient Nahuatl tradition, whose highest expression was reached in the Toltec world.

Castaneda makes his most detailed exposition of the tonal and the nagual in *Tales of Power*. There he reveals to us the two aspects of the tonal: as the space in which the aver-age person exists during the duration of life; and as the organizer that gives meaning and significance to everything having to do with awareness. The tonal includes all that a human is, thinks, and does, all that we can think and talk about. Reason, thought, and the ordinary description of reality are the fortress of the tonal, the entire spectrum of the known. It is noteworthy that for an average person there exists only the known, so that all conscious experience is restricted within the confines of the tonal, which begins at birth and ends in death.

The nagual then would be all that remaining outside the tonal. It is that about which it is not possible to think. Castaneda presents the tonal as an island upon which is passed the whole of life. No one knows anything about what lies beyond the borders of the island. The nagual would be all that space of unfathomable mystery surrounding it.

Although the nagual cannot be understood or verbalized—since understanding and words belong to the tonal—it nevertheless can be witnessed and experienced. That is one of the prime objectives of a sorcerer. It is not important to try to understand or rationalize the experience of the nagual; the sorcerer is interested only in the pragmatic possibilities it puts within his or her reach.

Although ultimately everything occurs in the nagual,

which is all encompassing, the task of the tonal is to endow
the reality of the nagual (the universe of the eagle's emanations) with order and meaning, which are not part of transcendental reality.

The tonal and the nagual aspects of the world also have a
corresponding expression in every human being, each of
whom has a tonal side and a nagual side. In the work of
Castaneda they are also called awareness of the right side
and awareness of the left side, ordinary awareness and
awareness of the other self, the *dreamer* and the *dreamed*. The
tonal, in giving order to the chaos inherent in the nagual, pro-
tects our being from the devastating impact that would result
were we to confront the nagual unprepared.

This distinction between tonal and nagual colors all of
don Juan's didactics, which are divided into teachings for the
right side and teachings for the left side. The first serve to
create more healthy and functional elements on the island of
the tonal or what is known as "sweeping the island of the
tonal" (IV-175). The second have the purpose of bringing the
apprentice to directly witness the nagual in such a way as not
to lose sanity.

So, if the tonal of each individual is what gives order and
meaning to the world, and the reality thus perceived has no
transcendental existence, then how is it that human beings
share a similar view of reality among themselves? What is it
that causes the tonal of every one of us to construct a reality
we all share?

Part of the answer can be found in what was said about
the collective construction of ordinary perception using the
first ring of power. However, there exists another factor
known as the "tonal of the times", which can be understood
as a general description of the world that the members of
each society share in their specific time and place. This they
sustain between themselves by having internalized it simultaneously and by transmitting it to the newly born within the
society. The latter must assimilate it to integrate themselves

as members, which they become the moment they are capable of reproducing and sharing said description. It is precisely the tonal of the times (IV-131) that imposes on each individual a description that, combined with the personal tonal, constructs a perception to agree with the rest of the members of the society. Naturally there exist small differences from person to person that have their origin in the individual personal history of each one.

THE AWARENESS OF THE OTHER SELF

On the left side, or nagual, of each person is what is known as "the awareness of the other self" (VI-313). Its rescue and reintegration into the reality of a person constitute one of the most commonly recurring themes in the work of Castaneda. In fact, the integration of the awareness of the other self with everyday awareness brings nearer the possibility of integrating "the totality of oneself" (IV-248).

While it is true that the awareness of the other self as an expression of the nagual is incomprehensible and its possibilities are practically unlimited, it is also true that throughout his work are presented many examples of its operation. Below are some of the aspects that lie hidden in the other self, aspects that can be experienced with the help of corresponding techniques as detailed in subsequent chapters:

- the "vague memories" of the other self include remembrances of our own past stored in the memory of the left side (other self) that are substantially distinct from those of ordinary memory. This refers to memories that were not in agreement with the description of the world so they were not registered by ordinary memory, thus remaining hidden in the awareness of the other self.

- the memories of our nature as luminous beings, which allow the perception of the human body as a field of energy.

- the awareness of our dreaming body, which allows the pragmatic utilization of our experience within the realm of *dreaming*.

- the awareness of our death, which is what gives the warrior the impulse and detachment necessary to respond in the most effective manner in any situation.
- the possibility to align ourselves with the awareness of other forms of life, organic or not, such as trees, animals, or the Earth itself.

It should be added here that in the work of Castaneda, the term nagual is also used to designate the leader of a party of warriors. This is the being who—thanks to an extraordinary level of energy—can generate the appropriate conditions necessary, thus allowing the warriors of the group to move their assemblage points and experience for themselves the separate reality located beyond the narrow confines of the tonal.

TWO

THE SEAL
OF IMPECCABILITY

THE MYTH OF THE WARRIOR

The warrior does not exist but is a myth—a beautiful myth of our time that, like all other myths, works to reflect our most noble aspirations as mortals. It serves as an invitation and a guide for the rare process of transforming ourselves into magic beings through their incarnation. All peoples of the Earth in all epochs have had myths that reflect their moral level and their inclinations. Myths are in fact a reflection of a society and the men and women who make it up.

Myths are, in part, stories told many times and transmitted from generation to generation. Anthropologically speaking, it would be absurd to question whether these tales are "real" or "fictional." Myths are real insofar as they serve a real function among the people of a society.

In its myths, a nation finds a mirror that reflects its best face and even its unknown face, the face of the *other*. That other that I am and nevertheless am not. That other that I am

19

not, yet dream to be. That other who is a reflection of myself, yet different: elevated, transfigured, converted into a being with power, magic, and above all, freedom.

The myth is the perennial hope of humans who, in spite of their faults, go on dreaming of the possibility of a life free of contradictions, free of oppression and violence and the maelstrom that make up a good part of life in society.

The myth is to society what dreams are to the individual. Therefore, the myth represents the dream of human beings, which whispers in their ear the promise of beauty and liberty.

From the myth of Christ, a man who through a life of purification and service was transfigured and converted into God, to the myths of Hercules, Quetzalcoatl, Wiracocha, Buddha, and many others, the theme is always the same: that of persons with profound aspirations living in a world of very low level ambitions; of the conflict between the society in which they live and the aspirations of their spirit; of the struggle with the doubts and the tests through which they must pass to finally achieve their dream: to transcend the chaos and miserable aspects of the human condition.

At the same time, myths also serve as a guide for action, a map by which we may arrive at the magical realities they describe. Far from being a form of entertainment, myths serve to promote methods of conduct and concrete action that permit us to leave behind the chaos in which we are accustomed to living.

When we do not prove ourselves equal to our myths and are consequently not capable of acting on them, we convert them into dogma and found a religion. When this happens, the myth loses its role as liberator and becomes, rather, an instrument of oppression. I would say that it ceases to be a myth. A myth is something to be lived, dogma is something to be believed; the first invites action, the second invites submission. The churches and their ministers serve as unnecessary intermediaries who generally obstruct our path—when they don't liquidate it altogether—toward liberty and knowledge.

Among so-called "primitive" peoples, myth and ritual are intimately linked. The rite or ceremony represents the time "outside of time." It is the space in which its participants will be transformed, incarnating the magic beings about which their songs and legends speak. This is the magic time in which the beings of power, light, love, and knowledge return to Earth to take on human form, the time in which humans convert themselves into the magic beings they dream to be.

I have lived that magic with the Huicholes, I have seen their ceremonial from the inside (since its meaning cannot be grasped from the outside): how the Marakame (the shaman) is transformed into deer-maize-peyote; how Tatewari (the grandfather fire) sings through his mouth and how humans are converted into little suns. It is not—as some believe—the mere fact of eating peyote that gives the Huicholes the power to incarnate their myths in the ceremonial. Anyone can ingest peyote or any other hallucinogenic plant, but it takes the trained, disciplined life of the Huicholes and a lifetime of training to make use of what they obtain upon having "a true vision" that reflects better ways of living.

In like manner, the "way of the warrior," in which the warrior represents a magic being living in the midst of everyday society, is a myth of our time. Not because warriors or men and women of knowledge do not have a concrete existence—for indeed they do. Rather this myth serves the same function as all others: to reflect our most worthy and dignified aspirations as mortals, inviting us to turn them into reality. Don Juan told Carlos that he could never become a man of knowledge (I-83). Similarly we never become warriors—at least not permanently—although we are always struggling toward that end, always on the path, like Genaro searching for Ixtlan (III-280).

For ourselves, the myth of the warrior is a marvelous invitation for its incarnation to become real within us. The attitude of a warrior begins by bringing a little of that magic time into our everyday lives: in place of acting like machines preprogrammed from outside, we choose to act purposefully in "the manner of a warrior". These moments of enlightenment in which we direct our lives from inside are like the magic time of a ceremony in which life speaks to us personally and we understand it. In which life becomes a friend. In which we comprehend what power and knowledge mean, not through imagination but through concrete events. The challenge for those who follow the way of the warrior is to work hard so that these magic moments in which the myth is incarnated become more frequent and continuous, until the magic predominates over submission and harmony over chaos. Until the dream of power and freedom predominates over the chaotic reality of everyday people. Until the dream becomes reality.

THE WAY OF THE WARRIOR: THE ONLY AID ON THE VOYAGE INTO THE UNKNOWN

Don Juan said in Castaneda's first book that a man goes to knowledge the same way he goes to war: with fear, respect, wakefulness, and with absolute confidence. Therefore, those who go to knowledge could very well be called warriors. The correct way to walk this path is in the manner of a warrior. In *Tales of Power*, the Yaqui sorcerer reveals that to live like a warrior "is the glue that glues together all the parts" (IV-235) of individual knowledge.

The spirit of a warrior is one of the central themes found throughout the work of Castaneda, and it constitutes the fundamental attitude required for the demands made by the path of knowledge. Don Juan tells Carlos that only as a warrior can a person survive in the sorcerer's world, although it is not necessary to be a sorcerer in order to be a warrior. The possibility is not easy, but it is open to anyone.

The way of the warrior of which Castaneda speaks has little or nothing to do with human wars such as we know them, principally because it has nothing to do with violence or the intent to destroy anything or anyone. Far from it, in fact. This is perhaps difficult to understand in a culture such as ours where the word "war" signifies one of the most frequent activities of "civilized" societies, whether it be on an individual or social level, and where it always refers to the intent to impose our will on others through subtle or outright violence.

However, the nonindustrialized world has known types of wars and conflicts far removed from war as we know it. An example of this would be the "flowery wars" practiced in pre-Colombian Mesoamerica that, due to their nonviolent nature, have never been correctly understood by Western historians. In fact, they have been regarded as merely another expression of war of the type with which we are so familiar.

The donjuanist point of view of the warrior and the struggle to be free is another example of a different type of war. The warrior is so called because he or she is always struggling against personal weaknesses and limitations; against the forces that oppose the increase in knowledge and power; against the forces that are driving us to our destiny as ordinary men and women, forces determined entirely by personal history and circumstances. The warrior wants to rescue the possibility to choose how to be and how to live. It is a struggle for harmony and tranquillity. It is a struggle for freedom, knowing that this struggle begins inside, projecting itself from there toward everything that makes up the world of actions. It a quiet, gentle, and joyful fight.

The way of the warrior is a form of constantly living the challenge of being; it eludes an exact or all-encompassing definition. The attitude of a warrior is a notion, a direction, a persistence in choosing the strongest and most authentic way in each action. Perhaps the most telling characteristic of a warrior is the perennial search for impeccability in every action, even the smallest. The warrior understands impeccability as giving the best in everything he or she does, which implies making optimum use of individual energy. Even when all other motivations crumble, the warrior will persist in acting impeccably, if just for the sake of impeccability alone.

Starting from this open concept, there arises an entire series of directives applicable to almost the entire range of human actions. Leading the sober life of the warrior gives a person the equilibrium and fortitude necessary to deal with difficult moments on the path of knowledge, regardless of the confusion suffered by reason or the injury caused to ego.

Anything that we do can be done in the manner of a warrior. A warrior is always in an unyielding state of total war, leaving no room for negligence or surrender. This transforms our smallest acts into a challenge of power to carry us beyond our limits each time, to be better, more powerful, more gentle, more real.

Among the fundamental elements available to a warrior, we can single out the will as a power that emanates from the self in order to touch and feel the world, even to direct it; a power that will have to be used in ever larger and more intense battles that we would not dare to confront using our reason. And now, warriors are no longer persons chained to the fears and fantasies of their thought; rather they pay attention to their feelings, moved by their personal power, that substantial energy that they have—through tremendous struggle—taken so long to increase and store.

Warriors also count on the awareness of their own impending death, performing each act as though it were the last battle and, therefore, the best. With death as a constant companion who infuses each act with power, they transform into magic their time as living persons on this Earth. The awareness of inevitable death endows them with the disinterest to be free from attachments while at the same time not indulging in denial. Detached from everything, conscious of life's brevity, and in constant struggle, warriors begin to arrange life through the power of their decisions. They work each moment to achieve control over themselves, thereby gaining control over their personal world. Warriors take the direction of life in their own hands and direct it strategically. Every little thing is an aspect of their strategy. In fact, control and strategy are two factors always present in their way of moving through life.

Control is the constant effort to intentionally and purposefully direct the different elements that fall into warriors' forms of being and living. They apply it to all that they do because their actions are not the result of chance, external circumstances, or emotional outbursts, but rather part of the strategy of a warrior's life. In it there is no place for whim or mechanical or impulsive actions, since warriors' actions are neither unconnected nor dispersed. Rather the actions adapt themselves always according to a previously planned strategy that warriors use to achieve the objectives that they have proposed as an expression of their most intimate predilection.

The elements that make up the strategy of warriors are the elements of the way with a heart, which allows them to derive enjoyment from each moment of time. Making use of will, control, strategy, and the awareness of impending death, warriors learn to reduce their needs to nothing. They realize that needs engender wants and misfortune. Hence, being free from need, there are no anxieties or worries. Warriors can act without the weight of need, anxiety, or unhappiness. When they cease to need, there is no compulsion, so they can involve themselves to any extent required. Free from need, all that they have and receive—even the smallest, simplest items—become marvelous gifts; and life, regardless of how much is left to them, remains in a permanent state of abundance.

PART TWO

THE SPECIAL
HANDLING
OF ORDINARY
REALITY

(PRACTICES FOR
THE RIGHT SIDE)

THE BODY AS
A FIELD OF ENERGY
OR
THE WAY TO
PERSONAL POWER

ENERGY

For don Juan as well as his apprentice Carlos, the world is not made up of solid objects, such as we perceive them, but rather of fields of energy—an idea in accord with the latest theories of modern physics. The idea of energy is one of the fundamental themes of donjuanist thinking and practice. It is fundamental not only because it appears frequently in his work, but because it also constitutes both the point of departure and the point of arrival for everything a warrior does.

Don Juan says that the world of desires or ideas has little real influence on the lives of people. Rather it is energy or personal power, the energy at our disposal, that determines everything: the possible and the impossible. As he says in

Journey to Ixtlan: "A man is no more than the sum of his personal power ..."(III-172).

LIGHT OR EGO?

In *The Fire From Within,* Castaneda alludes to a central theme that he calls "the mastery of awareness." He states that among its essential elements is the fact that we are, in reality, fields of energy or "luminous eggs". This may not appear to be a great secret, but within this idea exists one of the central elements that sustains the entire system of practices put forth by don Juan.

It is not difficult to comprehend that everything we do requires energy; not a single act can be accomplished without the necessary amount, be it running the Mexico City Marathon, breaking an old habit, or simply getting out of bed in the morning.

Although everyone has energy, we find that average people's energy is totally consumed in the routine acts of their lives, as determined entirely by their past. All of our energy in ordinary life is already invested within the confines of the known, leaving nothing for the exploration of the unknown. Any new undertaking on our part, if it is outside what we normally do, requires "free" or available energy to accomplish. This is the reason for the enormous difficulty facing an ordinary person wishing to change or to create situations distinct from those that make up the "normal" in his or her life: there is no energy "available."

On the other hand, anything undertaken on the path of knowledge will necessarily be concerned with energy. Warriors know that to venture into the unknown, with all the changes to be made, requires not only a high level of energy but also a high level of "available" energy. Thus, they examine everything having to do with energy. This is part of the secret of luminous beings. We are energy and all of our acts imply either a saving or a wasting of this life energy. Warriors know that each act either fortifies or weakens their energy and become very careful about the nature of their actions, striving always for impeccability, the optimum use of energy.

The key to the matter is this: if we stop perceiving ourselves as egos, accepting instead that we are fields of energy, then not only will we have to change the way we view reality, our way of behaving in it will tend to change as well. As egos we feel compelled to defend and reaffirm an enormous number of actions in the name of the ego; as fields of energy, on the other hand, our attention must be placed on how we use that energy, on whether it is increasing or decreasing. Therefore, our actions will tend to orient themselves toward the appropriate use of energy: *impeccability*, known also as the seal of a warrior.

As a simple and concrete example, take the case of a man whose ego reacts with frustration and anger because his wife did not have dinner ready when he got home from work. As an ego, he feels offended, since the ego demands worship and that everyone take as the truth all that he believes about himself. Therefore he will yell and threaten his wife, looking for her acceptance that the very important ego of her husband deserves to be treated with more consideration. If he gets it, she will cry, or beg forgiveness, or she will prepare dinner in a state of hurry and anguish. In a covert way she will be expressing to the ego of her husband (not his real self): "Yes, I believe you exist and you are real; I also believe everything you say and tell me about yourself is true."

Evidently this occurs because each time the ego fails to receive confirmation from external reality (as happen continually), it begins to have serious doubts about its own validity and therefore feels threatened. Thus it strives, through means endowed by personal history, to manipulate reality and the people around it until they are obligated to agree that the ego exists. It will become angry, offended, depressed, and even threaten suicide until it achieves the desired confirmation. Since it knows it has no concrete substance, it looks incessantly for confirmation from other human beings—those habitually occupied with similar matters—who accept and act as though the ego in question exists and represents the real person. Only in this way can the ego fool itself and make itself believe that it exists, although at heart it knows what it really is: a specific mass of nothing.

None of this can occur when we act in agreement with the knowledge of what we really are: a field of energy.

The man in our story would proceed in a different way if he were to perceive himself as a field of energy. As such, his first concern would entail the optimum use of his energy. He would know that anger consumes an enormous amount of energy while contributing nothing, save weakness, bad health, and poor quality of life, factors that do not constitute appropriate or desirable use of his energy. Thus in place of uselessly wasting his energy, he will consider his options: waiting quietly while dinner is prepared, or perhaps assisting in its preparation.

PERSONAL POWER

Don Juan's insistence that everything a person does or does not do, can or cannot do, that occurs or does not occur, depends on his or her personal power, is an idea congruent with the standard basic conduct of a warrior: *impeccability*. To say that warriors are always impeccable refers to their persistent search for the best possible use of their energy.

Concerning our nature as a field of energy, we can postulate the following basic premises:

- Everything living beings do, and everything that happens to them, is determined by their level of energy or personal power.
- The level of energy of all beings depends on three fundamental factors: the amount of energy with which they were conceived, the manner in which the energy has been utilized since birth, and the way in which it is being used at the present time.

- The form in which an ordinary person utilizes energy is not a product of chance or of choice; rather it is determined by his or her past.

- Although normally men and women consume all of their energy performing the routines dictated by their personal history, it is possible for them to make the following fundamental changes in their condition as fields of energy: redirect energy, save energy, increase energy.

- Everything that applies to human beings in relation to personal power applies to all living beings, since they are all fields of energy.

Everything living beings do, and everything that happens to them, is determined by their level of energy or personal power. Most of the time, ordinary people believe that the events of their life are determined by factors that are out of their control—because the events are physically removed from them, or because they are supposedly characteristic, intrinsically part of a person (ego). Thus we frequently hear people speaking of their bad luck as though it were something happening independent of themselves. They feel that events (especially those that are unpleasant) are against them because "someone" is doing something to them. Or if they assume the problems stem from themselves, they will speak of the things they can't control: "That's just the way I am." "I have no will power." "I have an explosive character."

In the same way, the enormous expenditure of energy involved in making unrealistic decisions, and in feeling despair when they are not carried out, is a phenomenon difficult to understand.

If I was so sure yesterday that I would get up and exercise, why don't I have the slightest desire to do so today? It is as though I am dealing with two different people. In a case like this, a person will usually say, "The trouble is, I have no willpower." And this explanation would not be so far from the truth if we understood "will" as it is understood by a sorcerer: an accumulation of available energy. An ordinary person nevertheless believes that "willpower" is a characteristic of personality that one either possesses or not, which cannot be developed "at will."

The thinking of don Juan is very different. Everything that happens to us depends on our personal power, and whether we have it or not depends entirely on ourselves: good or bad health, good or bad luck, available affection and love, doors open for us, doors which remain closed. Basically we can say that those who possess a high degree of energy lead sound, healthy lives (unless their energy is out of control), while the lives of those with a low energy level (the majority of humanity) will often be gray and painful. It would not be an exaggeration to say that those who have energy can accomplish anything, while those who lack it will always be poor—even though they may be swimming in material wealth.

THE ORIGIN OF PERSONAL POWER

The level of energy of all beings depends on three fundamental factors: the amount of energy with which they were conceived, the manner in which the energy has been utilized since birth, and the way in which it is being used at the present time. All human beings possess characteristics inherited from their ancestors, primarily the parents, although there are also characteristics from grandparents and farther back. The influence of ancestors is much less the farther one gets from the generation in question. This refers not only to physical, biological, or physiological characteristics but also to energy levels as well. We inherit both biological and "energetic" characteristics from our parents.

The first important factor is how much energy do the parents have, and second, how much of that goes to the new being they created at the moment of conception.

In a conversation with Carlos Castaneda, he told me that don Juan explained this very simply: if a person had been conceived with a great deal of passion, a large quantity of energy would be conveyed to the new being and he or she would be born "strong." On the contrary, if conception takes place among highly "civilized" people, perhaps after many years of marriage, with the television turned on or, as Carlos put it, is a product of "very boring sex," the level of energy at birth would be correspondingly low.

Fortunately energetic inheritance is not the only factor determining our energy level in life. It is also determined by how we use said inheritance, be it meager or plentiful. Thus those born with little energy but who make optimum use of what they have will be better off than someone with much energy but who lives out of control. In the first case, persons born with little energy—whether they express it to themselves in these words or not—start on the path of the warrior, which allows them to increase their level of energy. In the second case, people are born with a great deal of energy but have used it only to satisfy their whims and personal importance, which little by little wears away at their level of energy. These people get what they want with little effort, or manipulate with ease the people around them while giving nothing in exchange. They are accustomed to being loved but not to love. The same facility they have for satisfying their desires leaves them lazy and weak. They may be masters over the rest but remain slaves to their own weaknesses.

The ideal condition is: a lot of energy, perfect control, and sobriety. But in practice, more work is required than talent. There is no general rule, and in the final analysis results are determined not by initial energy levels but by individual effort.

It should be mentioned, while speaking of energy, that we must determine past and present uses of our energy and whether or not the two are connected. On one hand, "How much energy was I born with, and how have I utilized it all my life?" On the other, "How am I currently using my energy and what changes can I make?" One conclusion we can draw from the second question is that no one is condemned by the conditions of birth or past. We can change the use of our energy, restore it, or increase it.

DETERMINING THE PAST

The form in which an ordinary person utilizes energy is not a product of chance or of choice; rather it is determined by his or her past. Although we modern people like very much to consider ourselves free, in reality our possibilities of making a free choice are limited to only a very small part of our actions. Putting aside for the moment all functions and activities connected with biological conditioning, we find that the total remaining actions are determined entirely by personal history. Social class, nationality, sex, personality, religion, political ideology, complexes, and traumas, are only some examples of the many details that make up our personal history, thereby determining the what and the how of our daily existence. In reality when we believe that we decide, we are doing nothing more than setting in motion actions that have already been programmed into us by our past—exactly like a machine that does only operations for which it was designed. Thus are determined our beliefs, desires, choices, limitations, weaknesses, and talents. We don't choose with whom we talk or with whom we have relations, the places we frequent or those we avoid. Behind it all is our personal history, which is expressed through the structure of ego.

Ego and personal history are intimately related insofar as the first is the functional expression of the second. It is ego that daily compels us to sustain our personal history and act according to its dictates. Through this, said history is renewed and the resulting ego self-confirmed. We can only select from the options contained within the narrow limits set by the projection of our personal history through time.

From this we can conclude that the use of our energy as average people—the totality of our actions in other words—responds to a determination from our past in which the will normally does not intervene. Suffice it to say that the daily use of our energy in this manner is often very consuming and hardly gratifying—as we can see by merely looking at the expressions on people's faces in the street, in the subway, or trapped in their cars in a typical big city traffic jam.

HUNTING POWER

Although normally men and women consume all of their energy performing the routines dictated by their personal history, it is possible for them to make the following fundamental changes in their condition as fields of energy: redirect energy, save energy, increase energy. The possibility of *redirecting* energy seemingly contradicts what was established earlier—that our energy use is already predetermined by our past. If the use of our energy is predetermined, then how can this be changed? In reality, such a change is possible, although rare. The contradiction is resolved in practice.

Practice begins with a form of specialized conduct, actions that from the point of view of the ego are completely out of the ordinary. We might call them purposeful acts—or not-doings in no way connected to our past—which have the effect of opening little by little our field of possibilities. Through persisting in the performance of unusual acts, we create a disruption in the habitual patterns of our energy use, and as a consequence they begin to "loosen." Once this loosening process begins, we are in a better position to redirect the energy formerly spent in consuming activities toward new, much more worthwhile pursuits. In the moment we direct part of our energy toward less wasteful uses, an excess of energy is generated, which in its turn permits us to advance even more toward the redirection of our energy. This begins to express itself through the gradual increase of aspects of our life that pass from the realm of the impossible to the possible: giving up smoking or drinking, letting go of anger, taking time to listen to the songs of the trees or the messages of the birds. If we are persistent, our field of living and perceptual possibilities widens until the tendency to act in accordance with our personal history disappears. At this point, a person can be said to have erased personal history and is therefore free from its influence.

All of these changes are made possible, of course, by a certain level of energy. Change cannot occur without it. If we understand this, it will be apparent that for any new action to take place, we must find a way to increase our energy. This could be done by eliminating our most energy-consuming routines, then applying the energy saved to actions outside of those routines. However, if we occupy ourselves only with the redirection of energy without making an effort to save or increase it, we will achieve only limited results. The increase in personal power or available energy would appear to be the key to the whole matter. But nevertheless, it is not, at least not in principle.

Having come this far, we can see why it is not possible to undertake any unfamiliar or new action without having the necessary available energy for it. Since all of our energy is already apportioned out in accordance with the dictates of personal history, where can we obtain any extra energy? The obvious and immediate answer would be from the Sun and the Earth, our fundamental sources of energy supply. However, our relation to the Sun and the Earth is also determined by our personal history and is limited almost exclusively to the energy obtained through nutrition. We know that simply eating more will not give us more energy, although a better quality diet would help.

We generally do not know that there are other ways besides eating in which to obtain energy from the Sun and the Earth. We can also obtain additional energy directly from them through special exercises. Many cultures of non-European tradition have known and still know diverse procedures or rituals for achieving increased energy. Although I am familiar with some of these procedures (they will be presented in the following chapters), I must point out that they are useless if we do not have the necessary available energy to utilize them as true "connectors with the source." If we wish to have *more* energy, we must first have some energy available. This is what Jesus of Nazareth meant when he said, "For unto everyone that hath shall be given, and he shall have abundance; but from him that hath not shall be taken away even that which he hath." Again, we have a contradiction. This, however, will all be explained when we take into account the difference (already discussed briefly) having to do with energy, the difference between plain energy and energy that is "available."

We know that people possess varying amounts of energy. We also know that as average persons, all of our energy is consumed by the routines of everyday life. All of it! If we could somehow have more energy than we use, or simply use less than our normal amount, we would obtain then a supply of "free" or "available" energy. This energy could properly be called personal power—or that which is needed to perform actions outside personal history, including the gathering of energy directly from the Sun or the Earth, to live a freer life.

If in order to accumulate energy, we must have a supply of available energy, how can we obtain this primal energy? The answer is: we can *save* it. That's it. The way for human beings to obtain "free" energy is to save what they already have by not spending it on the routines of everyday life.

The method is simple but its effects are far reaching. If we suspend some of our internal or external repetitive actions, the energy thus liberated becomes available energy, which we can use to enter into the unknown—that which lies outside the dictates of personal history.

However, not all the actions of life can be suspended, and among those that can, not all are energy wasting. This is why warriors make an inventory of energy expenditures. That allows them to know, through the technique of stalking, how they use their energy and later to plan a strategy for redirecting its use; thereby they *increase* their available energy. From this inventory, apprentices can choose from their everyday activities those that are not indispensable for life and that are particularly wasteful and destructive (anti-energetic), to work for their temporal or definitive removal. Procedures for this will be outlined in the section on techniques. Naturally, effective suspension of our compulsive actions resulting from the force of personal history is dependent on having the necessary energy. This is particularly true in relation to habits, whether they be nutritional, emotional, psychological, or spiritual.

In practice, it can happen that the chosen activities— whose wasteful nature makes them appropriate for the practice of saving energy—are sometimes difficult to stop. We cannot stop them because we lack the necessary energy.

There is a way out of this apparently hopeless situation. It has to do with using what I call the "minimum space of personal freedom."

This "minimum" space of freedom constitutes areas of our lives—seemingly of little significance—in which it is possible to act purposefully outside of personal history. As average people we cannot, of course, immediately suspend such habits as smoking, anger, or self-pity. We can, however, change small things such as our sleeping position, or perhaps sleep on the floor. We can, for instance, observe for two weeks our first thought upon waking in the morning and our last thought before going to sleep at night; if we discover (as is usually the case) that they have a negative influence on our energy, then during the next two weeks, we can intentionally change these thoughts and think something different.

Working with an inventory of energy expenditures, it is possible to discover many small activities that allow us, right from the beginning, to save energy. Once this process has begun, the energy thus saved allows us to amplify our efforts to include a wider range of habits that were inaccessible earlier precisely due to a lack of energy. In this way, energy brings energy.

Examples of energy-consuming habits include: smoking, alcoholism, arguing, oversleeping, excessive thinking, judging others, criticism, condemning, complaining, identification with violent fantasies such as those seen on television, movies, or in the newspaper. Two examples that deserve separate mention are emotions and self-importance. These represent the two fundamental ways in which we consume our energy, and as we will see, they are generally related.

EMOTIONS

I will make a distinction between emotion and feeling at this point. This is much simpler than we might suppose: feelings are a natural reaction to what we perceive, while emotions are the product, not of perception, but of thought, of reason (which generally in the average person is not very reasonable). Feelings are not energy-consuming; emotions are to a high degree.

Our basic feelings of sorrow and joy arise from our simply being in the world. The body, for example, when it glimpses its final destiny, lets us know in the form of sadness or melancholy, which is neither painful nor energy wasting, but instead cures us of pettiness and restores our equilibrium. In a like manner, true joy comes from a place deep inside—not provoked artificially through jokes or comedy—and arises not through reason but through the direct perception of something that makes us joyful. We don't have to think to feel joy upon seeing newborn life, a hummingbird sipping from a flower, or a tree dancing with the wind, upon receiving a caress or an embrace.

Emotions, on the other hand, arise not from perception but from thought; they cannot be produced if we are without thoughts. Unfortunately, since we relegate perception to second place, our emotions put us in the situation of being able to manage our reality in a sensible way only with difficulty. Typical examples of emotions are wrath, jealousy, rancor, envy, self-pity, self-destructive depression. None of these emotions can be produced without the appropriate thoughts to accompany them. Who can become angry without thinking first? Nobody! In order to become angry, we have to tell ourselves that what someone did to us was unjust, that we deserved better, or something similar. If any readers have trouble believing this, then try to make yourselves angry without words or thoughts.

Consider the example of the lover who feels jealous when he observes his girlfriend talking and smiling with another man. Here are the simple facts: There is a woman (his girlfriend) talking with a man (a stranger) and she smiles. Are these simple facts what produces the energy-wasting emotion of jealousy? No! The lover, beginning with his personal history (perhaps he has seen too many movies, heard too many love songs on the radio, or witnessed the lack of love between his parents) upon seeing his girlfriend conversing and smiling, begins compulsively to talk to himself: "She has no reason to cheat on me. I should be the only person capable of making her smile. I never cheat on her, at least not so blatantly. She doesn't respect me." It is this type of thinking, not the facts themselves, that provokes the painful and energy-consuming experience of jealousy. It does not matter if in reality the woman is talking to her cousin, or a friend, or in fact has another lover; the jealousy emanates only from the imagination of the jealous boyfriend.

Once submerged in an emotional tidal wave, reality recedes further and further from us; the more we talk to ourselves, the less we perceive, and so on. So far from reality, how can we hope to handle it? We can become violent, making it easy to finish off the last traces of love or beauty that otherwise would have been present, and we still feel ourselves the victim. This is how we waste our energy. This is why it is worth the struggle to become a warrior.

Like the rest of our everyday actions, emotions are repetitive and are determined by personal history. Thus everyone has his or her own "emotional habits," each of which constitutes a personal way of wasting energy and of weakening the self. It is not difficult to discover, if we make a careful examination, that the conflicts and emotional problems of our lives manifest themselves in endless cyclical repetitions. Even if we change people and places, the problems are repeated time and time again.

This applies to all the emotions. They are pernicious and they create themselves.

Now we know a secret that if applied practically becomes a treasure of incalculable value: emotions cannot be produced without thoughts; what is more, they cannot be produced without the appropriate thoughts.

This puts us into direct contact with a way of saving energy. Should we find ourselves on the edge of an emotionally agitated state, we simply enter into a state of Inner Silence, and the emotion cannot then take place. If this alternative is not yet within our grasp, we can try changing the content of the internal dialogue. We could make a song using our thoughts for the words; put them in the form of a rhyme; think backwards or in a foreign language; go through the multiplication tables; or sing a nursery song. In each case the results will be the same: without the appropriate thoughts the emotion cannot be produced.

SELF-IMPORTANCE

Although in this chapter we will not be dealing directly with self-importance or ways to diminish or eliminate it, a few comments are nevertheless in order here, since, according to what the inventory of energy expenditures (see pg. 45) shows us, it generally consumes over 90 percent of our total energy, while giving nothing in return save perhaps illness, loneliness, weakness, and poor quality of life in general.

In effect, a large part of our personal energy is spent on activities related to self-importance that go far beyond vanity alone. Self-importance is the particular form in which our ego assembles and maintains its reality for its own self-confirmation and to convince itself it is real.

Without going into great detail at this time, we will look at some ordinary activities related to self-importance. The most extensive activities have to do with defense of the ego. Let us consider how much energy we consume. How much is spent in defending ourselves; in caring for our self image; in trying to influence the opinion that others have of us; in trying to be accepted; in defending ourselves against the criticism of others; in trying to demonstrate that we are the best, or that we are worth nothing, that we are the most beautiful, or the strongest, or the most miserable, most misunderstood, most sensitive, most cruel, most hurt—always the most something. How much importance we give ourselves! We live chained to what Castaneda calls "the mirror of self-reflection," one of whose principal characteristics is the self-image we project toward other people. And to this self-image goes the major part of our energy.

Therefore, eradicating or at least diminishing self-importance becomes a fundamental objective of a warrior, particularly the stalker. This process has nothing to do with morality; a warrior is not guided by moral abstraction but by impeccability. He or she is a field of energy and proceeds in accordance with that fact.

Although self-importance is a fundamental area relating to the saving of energy, the struggle and the techniques used to combat it represent the first of the not-doings of the personal self and will be explained in a separate section.

Everything that applies to human beings in relation to personal power applies to all living beings, since they are all fields of energy. Don Juan often referred to the existence of magical animals whose magic made them practically invulnerable; they were not likely to be captured by hunters. Their power was derived from the fact that—unlike ordinary animals—they had no routines. This endowed them with lightness, freedom, and extraordinary power. He said it would be fortunate indeed to encounter one of these beings.

So, in effect, the principle of personal power operates among animals as well. We could say that animals with "good luck" are those that have more energy. They live more intense and complete lives than their fellows. The same holds true for plants and other living beings. The energy of a tree, for instance, can be so powerful that simply resting in its shade or among its branches will produce a great, generally beneficent, effect.

In the same way, what happens among plants and animals also occurs among humans. Those who achieve a life free of routines and who have a high degree of energy transform themselves by right into magical beings who, at the least, do not follow the rules that govern the lives of the average person. Rather they rule their lives, destinies, and circumstances by this special power that is at their service, but that they also, inexorably, must serve.

TECHNIQUES

All that has been mentioned so far provides the basis for a nearly unlimited number of practical possibilities. However, before proceeding, I wish to make the following suggestion. The basic order in which these techniques can be practiced is: first from the perspective of saving energy, then of redirecting it and, lastly, of increasing it.

In order to save energy, we must begin to understand how and on what we normally spend it, which will allow us later to formulate a strategy for saving it. Therefore an inventory is the first technique we must practice, as a foundation for all the rest.

1. MAKE AN INVENTORY OF ENERGY EXPENDITURES

The general idea is to make a list that permits us to answer this question, "On what do I spend my energy?" A general answer would be that we spend it on all that we do, both internally and externally. Therefore, our inventory should consist of a list of all of our daily actions.

This is not an exercise of mental analysis or a reflexive process, which would simply be the ego giving a report about itself, justifying itself in the process, and therefore not yielding an accurate picture of reality. This is the exercise of stalking, which is based on observation. (It could be useful, however, to respond to the energy question by mental analysis simply to see which method gives a more accurate picture of reality.)

The following materials will be required:

- pen or pencil and a notebook.
- some kind of previously chosen signal, such as an alarm, that will call your attention at various intervals. Or you could have someone give the signal verbally, or you could remember every time you pass through a doorway, or any other signal that will wake you up at intervals and is more or less constant. (In the following exercise, I will assume you are using a watch with an alarm.)

Now perform the following steps:

1. Divide the pages of the notebook into three columns, heading them with the following questions in this order:

- What was I thinking?
- What was I doing?
- Is this what I want to do?

2. Set the watch to sound every fifteen minutes (or if the effect of the exercise is too strong, set it for every thirty minutes). It should go off at times other than on the hour, making it more unlikely that you will be able to anticipate the alarm.

3. Each time the alarm sounds, observe yourself in that moment and then respond in your notebook to the three questions. Don't analyze; simply record what you observe. The answers should be brief and concise. Also note the

time of the observation. Obviously, the questions refer to the moment prior to that of recording the answers. Try to answer them on the spot.

4. Before going to sleep, review what you wrote down during the day and respond in writing on a separate sheet of paper to the following questions:

• Were my thoughts varied or repetitive?

• What were the most often recurring elements in my thoughts?

• Were my actions varied or repetitive?

• Which ones were the most repetitive?

• Was there a relation between my thoughts and my actions?

• What percentage of my actions had anything to do with what I really wanted to do?

Answering these questions from the point of view of stalking will give you an idea of how you used your energy that day.

5. Repeat the procedure every day for one week. Then review the answers given to the three questions at the end of each day, using them to respond to the questions from step 4 but applying them to the entire week. This will show how you spent your energy during that week.

6. Repeat the procedure for four weeks, then again review your weekly answers, using these answers to respond to the questions in step 4 but applying them to the entire month. This shows how you used your energy during that month.

7. With that information, make the most detailed list possible of external actions (activities, routines, physical habits, addictions, etc.) and internal experiences (repetitive thoughts, emotional habits, illnesses, states of being, etc.) that make up your life. The resulting list becomes your inventory of energy expenditures.

8. Divide the elements of the list into two columns:

- That which is indispensable to sustain life (eating, sleeping, breathing, etc.).
- That which is not indispensable to sustain life (anger, criticism, jogging, drawing, etc.).

9. Divide the elements from the second column into two more columns:

- That which makes me feel well and/or that which I consider to be in my best interest to continue doing (sports, arts, a job that I like, making love, etc.).
- That which does not make me feel well and/or is not in my best interests to continue doing (reading the crime page in the newspaper, watching violence on television or in the movies, discussing illnesses, smoking, drinking, excessive talking, becoming angry, self-pity, trying to be accepted, etc.).

10. Divide the elements from the second column of step 9 into two more columns:

- That which is not possible to eliminate.
- That which can be eliminated either without difficulty or by making a small effort.

11. Select from the second column in step 10 a few elements that you consider appropriate and, during a specific period, cease to perform them. Immediately the energy that was formerly used for these acts will be converted into extra energy. At the end of your chosen period, decide whether you want to prolong the exercise indefinitely or suspend it.

Commentary on the technique

The act of observing tends to provoke very acute states of attention known as states of heightened awareness that can have many distinct levels. We should not be frightened by them since they are very useful.

Remember that the exercise of observation has to do with registering facts, not analyzing them, so be as coldly objective as possible when answering the questions.

It is a general condition for most people to have repetitious thoughts and habits around which their lives are centered. The modification of these would imply a complete change of life experience.

The criteria we use to define what is indispensable orwhat makes us feel well is highly subjective; therefore we should use our own criteria without too much worry.

To choose the actions to suspend, we can start with the easiest or with the most energy-consuming. It all depends on how intensely we are willing to work.

It is important to determine beforehand the exact length of time a given activity is to be suspended and it is best to make it short in the beginning. It is too taxing psychologically to think of quitting something "forever." To leave it for "a few days" is much easier. It also permits us to periodically evaluate our results and to decide whether or not to continue with the task.

2. TECHNIQUE FOR DETERMINING THE ENERGETIC QUALITY OF YOUR ACTS

Take a few moments to observe your body and sensations, or your spirit, after performing an act whose energetic quality you wish to know. The answer will be clear. If you feel good, vigorous, happy, and full, the act is energizing. If you feel weak, spent, out of sorts, and empty, the act is energy-consuming.

Commentary on the technique

In spite of its apparent simplicity, this technique can have far-reaching effects. These effects are never met with in ordinary life because normally we do not make an effort to observe ourselves (stalking) to obtain the information. Again, no analysis is required, only observation of what we feel.

All acts require the use of energy. Some even tend to function perfectly, to the point of increasing energy. They constitute, therefore, an appropriate use of energy, providing many benefits. Others only consume energy, causing us damage.

3. REFERENCES FOR DETERMINING YOUR ENERGY LEVEL
AT BIRTH

The exact method for determining the energy level you were born with is done through the exercise of recapitulation, which will be dealt with in another section. Nevertheless, you can get a general idea of it by briefly reviewing your past. Following are some indications to help determine this level; they can serve only as general guidelines, not as hard and fast rules.

High energy
- Restless child, curious, investigative, invents own games
- Popular with other children, a natural leader
- Independent child, does not need permission to act
- Attracted to the unknown
- A doer as an adolescent, involved in own projects
- Precocious in love
- Learned early to make money
- Popular with friends and with the opposite sex
- Healthy
- Left home early
- Lucky
- Successful

Low energy
- Timid child, asks permission for everything
- Tied to mother
- Afraid of everything
- A follower, not a leader
- Sickly
- Lazy as an adolescent
- Thinks a lot; rarely acts
- Little success with the opposite sex
- Never leaves home; must be thrown out
- Late in seeking employment
- Oriented toward failure
- Unlucky

Commentary on the technique

Naturally none of us is totally "energetic" or "anti-energetic" as these lists would tend to suggest; rather we find some characteristics in both columns. Predominance of one over the other gives us a general idea of our energy level.

People's energy levels vary according to how they have utilized it throughout their lives.

4. TECHNIQUE FOR STOPPING EMOTIONS OR DEBILITATING THOUGHTS

To stop debilitating emotions such as anger or jealousy is a simple procedure, but it requires discipline and a minimum amount of available energy. The key lies in our thoughts, the prerequisite for the production of an energy-consuming emotion. This technique works for any type of debilitating emotion.

There are two different techniques for this exercise: the first involves stopping the internal dialogue and the second—for those who yet do not have the necessary energy—involves its modification.

THE SEARCH FOR INNER SILENCE

Practice any of the techniques contained in the section on stopping the internal dialogue (chapter 6).

Modification

Change your debilitating thoughts into any of the following forms or invent your own:

- Without changing the content of your thoughts, make an effort to form them into a rhyme.
- Make a song using the contents of your thoughts.
- Think backward.
- Think in a foreign language that is unfamiliar to you.
- Assign a number to each letter of each word of your

thoughts, then add them up to determine the numerical result of your thoughts.

- Go through the multiplication tables.
- Recite a prayer from a religion that is not your own.
- Try to imitate the form of a well-known comic, using the contents of your thoughts as the material.

5. TECHNIQUE FOR SAVING ENERGY AND WELL-BEING

Practice strictly for a period of three days or more this golden rule: Don't criticize; don't condemn; don't complain.

Once the period is over, either begin another or wait awhile before beginning again.

6. TECHNIQUE OF SILENCE

Given that much energy is consumed in talking, stopping this activity can be very beneficial, especially for those who love to talk. Continue activity and interaction with other persons (talkers or not) during the execution of this exercise.

7. SAVING SEXUAL ENERGY

Sexual activity is a natural part of our existence, and normally human beings are born with enough energy to be sexually active for their entire lives. A more or less prolonged abstinence of part or all of our sexual activities can be an effective method for saving energy, principally because of the high grade of energy involved in sex.

Commentary on the technique

Sexual relations are not debilitating in themselves. What are debilitating are the things attached to the sex act, particularly in the Western world. Violence, repression, and guilt are some of the elements that can make a sexual encounter a negative energy-consuming experience.

Energetically speaking, abstinence is better than debilitating sexual encounters and healthy sexual activity is better than abstinence. The latter can open the way to increased perception and awareness apart from the enjoyment that it implies. Experiencing sexuality outside the ego and the mind can open the way to the unknown parts of our being and of reality. However, for this to occur, we must be free of obsessive desire[6] and guilt, both shackles that social hypocrisy uses to keep our bodies and hearts in chains.

8. CAPTURING ENERGY FROM THE SUN

In order for this technique to be effective, we must possess a certain amount of available energy and know how to choose the appropriate moment to create a connection.

Described here is a basic technique mentioned by don Carlos, the practice of which—with some variation—I have observed among indigenous peoples in Mexico.

Capturing the energy of twilight

The moment in which day and night come together had a high significance for don Juan since, as far as energy is concerned, it is a very appropriate moment in which to capture energy from the Sun. The technique is effective for sunset as well as for sunrise, but it usually functions better if we choose the one we are more naturally attuned to, according to the nature of our spirit. Personally I prefer sunrise, although my first experience was with the sunset.

1. Begin in a standing position. If practicing at dawn, you must begin before sunrise; if in the evening, a little before sunset. Look for a wide open area in which to have a clear view of the Sun. Direct your gaze toward the Sun, relaxed and attentive. Your arms are relaxed at your sides, palms facing toward the Sun. Your breathing is deep and concentrated.

2. At the moment of sunrise, begin to trot smoothly in place, being careful to deliberately increase your breathing as you increase your bodily movement. As the Sun rises, so does the intensity of movement and respiration. Raise

---

[6] A distinction should be made here between obsessive desire and natural desire. The first is a debilitating habit motivated by the internalization of the sick attitudes of our society toward sex. Natural desire, on the other hand, is a healthy impulse that motivates us to look for fusion in the mystery of the other person, beyond mind and structured experience.

your arms little by little with the palms toward the Sun,
concentrating on the sensation of heat; your movements
become more intense as the Sun climbs higher. When it is
completely above the horizon, your arms should be
extended in front of you, palms completely open toward
the Sun in an attitude of receiving energy. At this point,
your legs should be moving at maximum speed with
your knees raising as high as possible.

This exercise should be prolonged until it is finished,
which is understood to be any type of corporal "notice"—
such as a sensation of catharsis, an internal explosion, total
exhaustion, a burning sensation without pain, ecstasy, or any
other climactic experience. Stop at this point and remain
where you are until respiration and vital functions return to
normal.

Commentary on the technique

This technique may appear strange in our modern age,
but far from being an indigenous extravagance or something
similar, it makes use of universal processes in which the
human body, as a field of energy, establishes a peculiar form
of relationship with the source (the Sun or the Earth).
Phenomena of this nature can even, at times, be produced
spontaneously. An example of this is the first time it happened to me without a deliberate plan.

I was driving on the highway in the desert of southern
Baja California, hundreds of kilometers from the nearest
town. The Sun, high overhead, produced a stifling heat, miti-
gated only slightly by the air flowing through the open windows of the car. I stopped to relieve myself, a physiological
necessity after many hours behind the wheel.

I had hardly left my car when a peculiar sensation took
hold of me. I heard the murmur of the desert. Although I had
spent hours traveling through it, music from the tape deck as
well as the strain of driving had minimized the effect of the
singular force emanating from its desolate places.

Once relieved of my urgency, I was ready to resume my journey. I still had more than 250 miles to go that day to reach the next whale sanctuary.

In spite of my hurry, I paused for a moment to look around me. The sound of the desert is like none other. It gives the impression of a vibrating silence. The intensity of the Sun was suddenly diminished by some high altitude clouds. Everything took on a blue-gray hue. The vegetation around me consisted of low bushes and cactus typical of the desert. Far to the west, the distant mountains took on a dark blue color, but I was unable to determine whether they had vegetation or not. It occurred to me that hiking to those mountains would make an interesting excursion, walking in the middle of the desert. At that moment however, I had neither the time, knowledge of the region, nor adequate footwear to make the journey; it was just wishful thinking on my part. I turned to go back to my car.

Then something surprising happened. I became disoriented for a moment. My body began to walk toward the mountains while my ego, contemplating this new turn of events, asked, "Ah, so you are going for a walk in the desert after all? You know there's no time, besides it could be dangerous." To which another part of me replied, "Only for a while; just to take a little stroll." Meanwhile, without paying any attention to this dialogue/monologue of my mind, my body kept on walking. As I was walking, a kind of comforting heat took hold of me; it made me feel secure and at peace. The sweat of my body was refreshing. The mountains remained as far away as ever. I knew I wouldn't be able to reach them, and with that knowledge, I was able to keep on walking without worry, thinking that I could return to my car any time I liked. As a result of the work that my body was doing, I eventually reached a point where my ego was silenced. When I stopped thinking, nothing mattered—only walking for the joy of walking. The mountains now appeared closer. Thoughts began to return again for short moments, saying that the mountains were still far away and there was no need to reach them. At one moment, I looked back for my car and it had disappeared, along with the highway. Then the silence took hold of me again and I kept on walking. I felt the fascination of the desert and as I walked, I was transformed into nature. I was not moved by any impulse; I simply found myself there and the only thing I could do was to walk. With each step, the mountains attracted me more and more, growing in size as I approached. I did not know if I would be able to reach them, but since it didn't matter whether I arrived or not, I kept on walking—just one step more, just one step more. The diminishing sunlight made me aware of the passage of time. It was almost dusk when I found myself at the foot of one of the mountains. It appeared very high and, from where I was standing, formed an enormous, almost vertical cliff composed of a soft, unstable type of rock that crumbled very easily. I had arrived after all, without having made a conscious decision to do so. I had accomplished what hours before I had thought impossible. I thought, "Well, now that I am here, I will climb just a little to have a better view of the countryside." I began to climb, or to be more precise, to scale, the rock wall, feeling as though I were a puma in its natural habitat. A feverish anxiety took hold of me. I knew something awaited me up there and I felt the need to reach the top before dark. I did not know what I was looking for, but the impulse was very clear. The hours of walking in the desert had put me in a very receptive state of increased sensitivity, and I knew—without the use of my reason, which in this moment would only have served to terrify me anyway— what I had to do. Now and then I looked down and saw how high I had climbed; one error, one false step and I would never leave this place alive. Nevertheless, I felt happy, my body more awake with each step.

I arrived at the top of the enormous wall and discovered that beyond it lay the true summit, invisible from the base. The distance to it was greater, but its slope was much less steep. Without thinking, I began to run toward it.

I reached the summit just at twilight. I had a few moments to contemplate the world, the solitude, and the free reign of nature, very far from the world of human affairs. In front of me, beyond the enormous desert, I could see the Sea of Cortes. Turning around, I saw more desert and the Pacific Ocean. I felt as though I were on top, not of the everyday world but a magical and mysterious world that was peaceful and harmonious and, at the same time, potent and powerful. I became aware of my insignificance in this immensity. I knew that I was neither more or less important than everything that surrounded me, and I felt happy. I recalled the concerns of my everyday world and they seemed small in the face of this vastness. I turned toward the sunset. The world took on a dark blue coloration, within which the sky, sea, Earth, and my own heart were fused together. Suddenly, I felt something well up from the Earth under my feet, come up through my legs and spine to my head, like a ticklish sensation or an electric current—a tension that obliged me to move. The energy increased in intensity as did the speed of my movements. The Earth was teaching me a secret. Without any conscious plan on my part, I found myself frenetically running in place with my arms extended and my hands open, palms toward the Sun, raising my thighs in an uncontrollable tremor. Tears ran down my face. The world turned red. Something burst inside me and I felt liberated. I knew the next step of my task in this world and I felt complete. The mysterious had opened a window and I had taken a look at my destiny. I accepted it with joy.

In the darkness, full of energy, with a kind of light emanating from my body, I descended the mountain and walked back across the enormous desert to my car.

FOUR

THE ART
OF STALKING
AND ITS PRACTICE

STALKING AND THE SEPARATE REALITY

According to the donjuanist vision of reality, there exists a separate reality that is parallel with our ordinary reality. One fundamental aspect of the task of warriors is to reach this alternate reality, which will allow us to experience our world in its totality.

In general terms, the perceptual velocity needed to be able to perceive this separate reality can only be achieved by a movement of the assemblage point (see page 9). As has already been mentioned, this tends to be permanently fixed in place during the life of an average person. Lacking this movement, we remain anchored to the generally chaotic conditions of our ordinary reality.

The separate reality, on the other hand, invites the warrior to freedom. It offers new worlds full of mystery, in which each being can experience itself in unsuspected ways. Don

Juan outlines two general ways in which to achieve movement of the assemblage point: the art of *dreaming* and the art of stalking. In the present chapter we will deal exclusively with the art of stalking.

THE CONTROL OF CONDUCT
IN THE EVERYDAY WORLD

The art of stalking takes place within the reality of the everyday world. It is practiced in right-side awareness; that is, it consists of an extremely careful and specialized handling of ordinary reality, with its final aim the penetration into this separate reality. The stalker is a consummate practitioner who makes the everyday world a battleground in which every act, every interaction with fellow humans, forms part of the strategy.

Stalking is the strategic control of our own conduct. Its field of action is the interaction that takes place between human beings (warriors or not). Therefore the stalker, far from fleeing from the social scene, immerses himself or herself in it, using it to temper the spirit, gain energy, and carry the self beyond the limits of personal history.

STALKING AND HUNTING

The term "stalking" naturally reminds us of hunting. A stalker is one who observes, one in whom stealth forms an integral part of conduct. A hunter is necessarily a stalker, although only warriors would be able to apply this technique to every aspect of their life, converting its every element, including self and personal weaknesses, into their prey, .

The true hunter, as well as the stalker, well knows the difference between judgment and observation, between paying attention and thinking. If we wish to trap prey, we must first observe it. We must silently perceive what the prey does in order to know its routines: where it eats, when and what time it sleeps, its movements, and so forth. If our observation is

effective, we will become familiar with these routines, allowing us to later devise a trap against them.

The average person, unable to distinguish between
thoughts and reality, confounds observation with judgment.
We pass through life thinking things (generally negative)
about the people around us, or about ourselves, and this we
call observation. The observation of the hunter, however, has
nothing to do with criticism. Imagine for a moment what
would occur if hunters, instead of observing the prey silently,
begin to speculate about its qualities or defects, judging it as
beautiful or ugly, interesting or boring. For example, in place
of observing where and at what time it drinks water, imagine
saying to yourself: "I imagine that this animal is accustomed
to being thirsty around noon, and, therefore, it will have to
drink water at the water hole; besides it has a foolish looking
face so it shouldn't be difficult to trap." Later, having taken
your thoughts seriously, you are angry that your is prey far
from the water hole at midday.

When hunters observe, there is no room for thought or
internal dialogue. Everything is direct and simple: merely
observe what is there. Observation is one of the basic elements upon which the art of stalking is constructed. Another
one is unusual behavior.

STALKING AND THE ASSEMBLAGE POINT

In *The Fire From Within*, don Juan tells us that the internal
dialogue itself, together with everyday conduct, is what
keeps the assemblage point fixed in one place. Then, any
unusual conduct, if practiced continuously and systematically, tends to move it out of this habitual position. While it is
true that there are many ways to move the assemblage point,
it is also true that many of them can put our mental health in
danger, since we are already disposed to believe that the reality we perceive is the one true reality. Examples of this would
be the careless use of hallucinogenic plants or confrontation

with a severe emotional crisis that leads to psychosis. Even in the work of Castaneda, we find Carlos, the sorcerer's apprentice, concerned about going crazy from the effects of power plants or from the celebrated "nagual's blow".

Stalking, on the other hand, implies a systematic control of our conduct, allowing a slow and harmonious movement of the assemblage point. We are thus assured that any contact with the unknown will be carried out with sobriety and efficiency.

STALKING AND SUCCESS

The stalker's method is also the most efficient way to interact with people in everyday society. Since stalkers' moves are based on what is observed, not on what is thought, since the perception of reality widens with the movement of the assemblage point, since all acts are motivated by strategy instead of whim, they find themselves in a superior position in the realm of human affairs with respect other people.

Most people think in terms of a separate reality—assuming they even conceive of its existence in the first place—in wild or phantasmagoric terms. They imagine a world of allies and beings that walk on walls. In actual practice, penetration into other realities might include experiencing unusual psychic phenomena—such as the *dreaming body*, communication without words, or perceiving living beings as "luminous eggs". It also can include the realization that we are not condemned to live our lives under the yoke of our egos, that it is indeed possible to reinvent ourselves. We realize we can create new and more healthy ways to love; that the order we want in our personal world can be found within ourselves—not influenced by external factors such as inflation, world crises, or the opinions of others.

All of this is especially relevant to the art of stalking. Its practice endows us with very powerful tools for operating more efficiently in everyday society, propelled and sustained by an impulse that comes from somewhere else, from the *otherness*. This force, properly directed, can ultimately be devastating in a world where people are only familiar with the right side of reality.

In summary, the art of stalking is observation, strategic control of our acts, stalking the self, the most efficient control of matters in the everyday world, and achieving movement of the assemblage point while maintaining sobriety and efficiency. It is the establishment of a bridge from this side of reality to arrive at the other self.

STALKING IN THE WORK OF CASTANEDA

The art of stalking forms one of the two great axes around which revolve the entire system of ideas presented in the work of Castaneda (the other being the art of *dreaming*).[7] Any attempt at defining it would prove fruitless, first, because it cannot be understood through reason; second, according to statements made in two of his late works[8], his writings—particularly that portion dealing with the mastery of stalking—remain incomplete. Only if one has a personal understanding of stalking can its importance within the totality of the ideas presented by Castaneda be fully appreciated.

Nevertheless, I will try to summarize here the principal concepts of the art of stalking as they are dealt with in Castaneda's works. These concepts are not included in the technical portion of this book (even though don Juan and later Florinda insisted on such concepts as pragmatic guides for action) principally because the result would be far too general and lengthy. I quote them here for the benefit of readers who may not have copies of Castaneda's works at hand, so they may better comprehend and apply the many stalking exercises that are included in the following section. The same comments apply to the "stalker's strategy" (VII-31) mentioned in the technique of the "petty tyrant".

---

[7] See bibliography of Castaneda books in the appendix.
[8] *The Fire From Within* (1984) and *The Power of Silence* (1988).

PRECEPTS OF STALKING (VI-279)

- The stalker realizes the world is an endless mystery.
- The stalker must try to unravel this mystery, realizing that there is not the slightest possibility of doing so.
- The stalker regards him- or herself as a mystery as well.

PRINCIPLES OF STALKING (VI-278–291)

1. Always choose your battlefield.
2. Eliminate all nonessential elements.
3. Consider every battle a life or death struggle.
4. In difficult situations, relax, abandon yourself, while fearing nothing. Only then will the powers that guide you open the way for you.
5. Do not allow yourself to be overwhelmed. When you encounter forces greater than yourself, retreat for a moment, and let your mind wander.
6. A stalker compresses time; even an instant counts (VII-281).
7. Never show your hand; a stalker is never direct with anybody.

THE FOUR MOODS OF STALKING (VIII-87–88)

Ruthlessness—begins by not having compassion for yourself and is applied to all aspects of your life. Compassion is nothing more than another facet of self-importance. Ruthlessness has nothing to do with coarse behavior, however.

Cunning—relates to a type of sagacity that is closer to intuition than to intelligence. It does not imply cruelty, however.

Patience—does everything in its proper time. There is a right moment to take action. You must be patient but active. It is not negligence, however.

Sweetness—is not taking yourself too seriously. The power to laugh at yourself permits you as a warrior to be gentle, charming and, at the same time, an annihilator. It is not to be confused with stupidity.

RECAPITULATION:
THE STALKER'S STRONGHOLD

According to don Juan, recapitulation is the stronghold of stalkers in the same way that *dreaming* constitutes the stronghold of dreamers, and it can be considered the basic practice that makes one into a stalker. Recapitulation is remembering, or, more precisely, reliving. It is the bodily recovering of all past experiences.

I consider recapitulation a fundamental technique for anyone—warrior or not—who is genuinely interested in self-liberation. For this reason, recapitulation is one of the first techniques I give to those participating in my workshops. I consider it—by itself—to be one of the most significant techniques in terms of its permanent repercussions in the lives of those who practice it.

In don Juan's terms, recapitulation is a very effective way to move the assemblage point, thereby connecting awareness to the other self.

THE RECAPITULATION OF A DYING PERSON

Recapitulation is a natural act. It is the last act of living beings just before the disintegration of their individuality, which is death. It happens to everyone just before the moment of death.

People reviving after being declared clinically dead often will report that their "whole life passed before them." This is not so absurd; we are because we remember. Our capacity to associate and remember is what gives us our sense of individual identity and continuity. It is natural that in the moment just prior to ceasing to be, we would remember all those events that caused us to identify ourselves as ourselves during our life. This is the moment when our "I", in taking its leave, enjoys reliving for the last time all that it will no longer be able to remember, all that will no longer be. This experience of reliving the events of life is recapitulation. Those rare people who revive possess an increased capacity to appreciate their existence, living with a better sense of equilibrium, force, and decision making than they had before. This is due not only to having been so close to death—which without doubt nourishes an awareness of life—but also to their having made a partial recapitulation of their lives.

THE BURST OF AWARENESS

Castaneda states that once the body has completed its final recapitulation, a burst of total awareness occurs that lasts only for an instant before death itself—or what he calls the moment in which the eagle consumes the awareness of the dying person. For only an instant—thanks to recapitulation—at the moment of death, we become pure awareness.

Stalkers have a very keen interest in the super awareness derived from recapitulation, and they ask, "Why wait for the moment of death to recapitulate? Why not recapitulate before and make use of its power to change our lives now?" This is precisely why recapitulation forms the basis of stalking.

Discovering recapitulation as a means of liberating and developing awareness has universal value. It is not something that has to do only with sorcerers, stalkers, or strange entities. It is not done simply because we all are going to die and we all are going to recapitulate. The effects of recapitulation are too far-reaching to be ignored.

BODY MEMORY

I want to make clear that recapitulation does not refer to ordinary memory. Recapitulation is the not-doing of memory. While ordinary memories deal only with thoughts, recapitulation is more like a sense memory having to do with feelings. When we remember, it is the ego remembering by means of the internal dialogue, to which we add images. In recapitulation, on the other hand, it is the body remembering and it does so by liberating the feelings stored within it.

The vast majority of us are tied to our past, which is to be expected since it provides the support that the ego uses to justify itself. The past determines what we are and makes us feel justified in maintaining our everyday behavior even though we may be aware that it is not good for us. A large part of our time is spent remembering the past. Only we don't realize that what we are remembering is not reality but rather images fabricated by our internal dialogue concerning what happened to us. We don't remember facts but interpretations of facts. We are unaware of our real past because we are too involved in repeating to ourselves a mythical history that our ego has developed to justify its existence.

Nevertheless, the awareness of what we have lived and done is not totally lost. We possess an alternate memory hidden in the awareness of our other self, which has nothing to do with the interpretations of the ego, and which it is possible to recover. Recapitulation is a bodily experience contained in the totality of our being that allows us to relive the feelings implicit in the events being recapitulated. The information it provides generally does not coincide with what our ordinary mental memory says about our own existence.

THE FAILURE OF PSYCHOANALYSIS

Allow me a very brief digression to discuss psychoanalysis. It often happens that when I speak of recapitulation, cultured people who are unfamiliar with it immediately associate recapitulation with psychoanalysis.

Some of them say, "Ah yes, I have recapitulated already for three years with my psychoanalyst." Perhaps secretly they ask themselves, "Then why haven't I changed?" The reason is that recapitulation and psychoanalysis are two entirely different practices. The first has to do with left-side awareness, the second with right-side awareness. The first comes from the body, the second originates in the internal dialogue. Recapitulation is the reliving of experiences, psychoanalysis is an interpretation fabricated by thinking which we call the past. In psychoanalysis the ego of the patient, talking a great deal about itself, reinforces its belief in its existence as time goes on. Thanks to this self-justification, it affirms its place as the dominating force in the totality of the patient. Naturally, this is satisfying to the ego of the analyst who—upon observing a certain prescribed behavior from the patient—feels he or she is indeed an analyst, thus justifying all those years of study at the university. And, of course, the fee for such lengthy therapy would be no small matter either. Result: a patient who spends years as a patient, suffering in the same existential wretchedness, but capable of explaining with complete precision the cause of his or her problems. Unfortunately, the patient remains incapable of changing anything.

If it is clear that recapitulation does not involve ordinary memory and it is the body and not the mind that carries it out, we can now discuss its effects. These include personal freedom, increased awareness, and an increase in energy.

THE CHAINS OF THE PAST

Some have asked during recapitulation exercises in my workshops, "Why bother with our past when what really concerns us is the present? Haven't we been told to live in the here and now?" These questions bring up a very important point concerning recapitulation: we are not dealing here with events that happened a long time ago, but with a past that is still in effect right now. These past events are still registered on our bodies, and are in fact determining everything that we are and do. They determine our way of thinking, which things are easy for us and which things we find difficult, our strong and weak points, people who attract us and those we avoid, our way of dressing, our way of loving and experiencing affection—in short, all those characteristics that would be included under the headings of "Who I am" and "The way in which I live."

Therefore, recapitulation is not remembering something

that was and is no longer. Rather, it represents an encounter with something that continues to operate in us right down to the present moment, profoundly affecting each instant of our present life. Here and now, each person is tied to other persons, to an unlimited number of places, objects, and situations that are not apparent at first glance. All of these ties are in reality filaments of our luminosity that remain attached to those people, places, objects, and situations throughout our lives. Therefore, when we want to move, change, intend, or undertake something really new in our lives, we find we can't. We drag these attached filaments behind us like an enormous weight that keeps us fixed in our old routines, our old ways of living. The people with whom we interact may be different ones, but the events will repeat themselves.

A DOORWAY TO FREEDOM

From this it can be deduced that recapitulation also represents a doorway to freedom. If we can know directly, without interpretations, how this ego was formed, what things we renounced, what promises from the past we secretly drag along behind, how it is that we come to believe who we believe we are; if we are capable of perceiving ego as a description fabricated during past stages of life, which therefore is not as real or definite as we had previously supposed; then it means we are capable of change. It means we are not condemned by this vulgar history called our past. This implies that if we know what our structured routines are, then we have the necessary information for determining which not-doings would be the most appropriate for dismantling them, for erasing our personal history. We can then choose how to live and how to be, in what type of world we wish to live. We can abandon repetition and boredom and replace them with magic, amazement, and joy.

RESCUING YOUR QUASI MEMORIES
OF THE OTHER SELF

In *The Eagle's Gift*, when Castaneda refers to the "quasi memories of the other self," we are apt to imagine that such a thing—if it exists at all—would have to do only with sorcerers or some sect or cult. It surely would have no relevance at all in the experience of the average person. In that work, Castaneda relates how, after enormous efforts, he recovered his memories of long chains of events that took place while he was in a state of heightened awareness but that were not contained in his ordinary memory. These experiences were contained in the awareness of his other self. Only through great effort on his part was he able to recover these quasi memories of his other self. Remembering the magnitude of these events that had such a profound effect on his life provoked an enormous upheaval in him that left him stupefied, exclaiming, "How could I have forgotten something so tremendous?"

The reality is that each of us as a human being has our own quasi memories of our other self. These are not experiences with sorcerers in states of heightened awareness, of course. They refer to profound, definitive experiences in the past for which (as in the case of Carlos) the only relief was to forget them completely. When the ego runs up against something that does not fit with its description of the world or of the self, the trauma can be so great that it simply discards the experience or somehow explains it away. Those who recapitulate their lives, then, express the same perplexity as Castaneda: "How could I have forgotten that?"

They forget because the events that occurred were not impressed upon ordinary memory but upon the parallel memory of the other self, whose report about their existence would be quite different from that of their ego. In some part of our body (taken as a field of energy) are hidden the quasi memories of our other self. In these memories are the mechanisms that close the way to many of the experiences that we long for but that appear to be out of reach. Promises made are an example of what might be found in quasi memory.

THE PROMISE

A clear example of "the promise" is given in *A Separate Reality* when don Juan forces Castaneda to remember a promise that had been forgotten in his ordinary memory but which nevertheless continued to exert its force on his life. It had to do with the little boy "with the button nose" (II-147).

As a boy, Carlos had to wage great battles against other children, the kind that many children wage against the cruelty and mockery that often characterize childhood relationships. These are the battles that determine who is strong and who is weak. With great effort, Carlos achieved supremacy, becoming one of the strong ones who made fun of and dominated the other children. One of his favorite victims was little Joaquin, a first grader whom Carlos picked on frequently without really being aware of it. In spite of this, Joaquin had a great admiration for Carlos and followed him everywhere. On one occasion, Carlos went too far: he deliberately toppled a heavy blackboard over on his little admirer, breaking Joaquin's arm in the process. The impact of seeing little Joaquin on the floor crying, with fear in his eyes, and not understanding the reason for it all, shocked Carlos into promising himself that if little Joaquin were healed, never again would he be the dominator. Until don Juan forced him to remember this event, Carlos had unknowingly carried the weight of his promise around with him.

All of us have similar "promises" hidden away in some part of our being. Discovering them, knowing them, provides us with an opportunity to determine whether such promises are still relevant or whether it is time to rid ourselves of them.

Recapitulation is the best means of accomplishing this, to reencounter our quasi memories of our other self. It represents an opportunity to know who we truly are.

SEALING BLACK HOLES

The most important effect of recapitulation is increasing our energy. In the multiple interactions we have with other human beings, we experience painful moments in which we lose parts of our luminosity. Particularly in a strong emotional exchange, we experience a great loss of energy as complete parts of our luminosity fall off and are left behind. After such interactions, we never again feel complete, secretly feeling we lack something, although we are not sure what it is. Using don Juan's terminology, we would say that "holes" form in our luminous egg through which energy is continually being drained and wasted, thus weakening our equilibrium and power. That these energy holes are a constant drain can be observed in the lives of average people; there is a tendency to repeat the debilitating routines that began with some painful emotional exchange—that is, starting from the formation of one of these holes.

A common example of this happens in the separation of lovers. The abandoned partner feels as though a part of the self is lost. There is a physical pain in the umbilical region of the abdomen. This is not allegorical. In Western society, the tendency toward possessive love produces such a strong bond in the luminous fibers between the partners that any separation results in the mutilation of at least one partner, so that person would probably remain feeling incomplete forever. And as we know little about love—being concerned instead with property—so also we know little about life, and we are not in the least concerned with the fact of our inevitable death. We are so ill prepared to know about our own death that when it comes something will be torn from us similar to what occurs in the separation of lovers.

Recapitulation permits the recovery of energy lost along the way by providing us with the means to plug the holes in our luminosity.

However, as we leave shreds of energy tied to past moments, places, people, and situations in our lives, so other persons have left part of their beings in us. They have left their mark on us, and by this they can disrupt our time and space regardless of whether they are present or not, alive or dead. Because of this, many times I am not myself. I am someone else—my father, my mother, my kindergarten teacher, my best friend from long ago, an old love, or someone else. As I lose parts of my being to others, I also carry parts of others along with me, which prevents me from living a full life. Don Juan stated that these "foreign" filaments also form the basis of our capacity to feel important (VI-289).

Detaching these fragments unconsciously incorporated into our being is also achieved through recapitulation.

TECHNIQUES

Since it is applicable to everything we do, the art of stalking encompasses an inexhaustible wealth of activities. I will, however, confine myself here to some of the basic exercises. The first three have to do with recapitulation and the other six relate to other forms of stalking.

Recapitulation procedures

There are many ways to recapitulate—while buried in the Earth, with the help of trees, with another person, in a group, through massage, or through physical movements in a group. In our work groups, we have used several different techniques.

The basic procedure for recapitulation is presented to us by Castaneda in *The Eagle's Gift*: recapitulating inside a box. I consider this to be the most efficient and complete technique for general recapitulation.

First let me clarify that exercises of recapitulation and recapitulation proper are not the same. Exercises of recapitulation can bring us to recapitulate, but they do not in themselves constitute recapitulation. True recapitulation comes from the body without the help of any method or procedure. It has its own dynamics according to the way the body handles itself as a field of energy. There are even situations in which people in physical trauma or other types of crisis experience spontaneous recapitulation without their having realized it.

The following is a systematic procedure to help the body to remember and in this way to achieve a general recapitulation of your life.

The recapitulation box

Using a box for recapitulation requires three elements:

• A list of events to recapitulate.
• Special breathing techniques.
• The recapitulation box.

Each of these elements constitutes a separate technique in itself; however, maximum effect is reached when they are used together.

In very general terms, the procedure is as follows:

1. Make a list of all the events of your life beginning with the present and finishing with the most distant, the event of your birth.

2. Enter the box and, by means of special breathing, recapitulate one by one each event, from the present to the past.

It seems simple at first glance. However, in actual practice, each element constitutes a technique involving a high degree of complexity, as we shall see shortly. I will develop it element by element and then clarify how they are interconnected.

9. THE LIST OF EVENTS

This technique involves a written list of the events we are going to recapitulate. In theory this list should include all the events of our existence, beginning with the moment in which stalkers begin writing the list and finishing with their birth or before (recapitulation can include prenatal experiences). Naturally, such a list would contain a practically inexhaustible number of events—the universe of our past would be too enormous to be functional. In practice, we begin to work first with the most significant events and those that spring readily to mind.

Don Carlos himself suggests that we recapitulate our life by dividing it into areas. The information contained in his work, personal suggestions from Castaneda himself and, above all, the practical application of the exercise, permit us to fine tune this extremely simple method that consists of the following steps:

1. Select three areas of your life to recapitulate.

2. Divide each area into its component elements.

3. Divide each element into stages.

4. Divide each stage into its specific events.

Areas. Choose areas that have to do with things or activities that have been with you for a good share of your life. Typical examples would include: "Houses in which I have lived," "love relationships," "my family," "my friends," "my work," "schools." The important thing is to be able to break the chosen area down into its elements. Choosing "houses" would be of little value if you have lived in only one house your entire life, or choosing "lovers" if you have never had one.

Areas give you a sort of cross section through time, allowing you to chart your entire existence without examining all the details. You can do without any events that do not readily appear in relation to a selected area.

Elements within a given area. These are the specific units of the area listed one by one from the present to the past.

If my chosen area was "houses," I would begin the list with the house in which I currently live, then the house I lived in just before, and so on to my very first house.

HOUSES

1. Vallarta 49, D.F. (where I currently live)
2. The house in Azulejos, Veracruz (the house immediately prior to number 1)
3. Grandmother's house (prior to number 2)
4. Such and such house (prior to number 3)
5. And so on and so forth until I arrive at—19 (the house of my birth)

If the chosen area has to do with persons, such as lovers or family, try to list its elements (names) in reverse time order as in the example above.

Stages within a given element. This step can appear to be the most complicated, although it isn't really. Divide into stages each one of the elements beginning with the one at the top of the list and follow the same order from present to past. The most helpful method is to name each stage according to an event that in some way marks the beginning of the stage. To continue with my example:

1. VALLARTA 49

1.1 The recapitulation list (current stage)
1.2 The books of Castaneda (from one year ago to the present)
1.3 Remodeling the house
1.4 Grandfather's illness
1.5 Arrival at Vallarta 49

The names given to each stage are not taken as the events themselves but as points of reference to orient yourself within some specific element. The time frame may vary a great deal in each case. The number of stages can vary depending on the time spent in a given element; however, it should never be less than three. Between five and ten is usually sufficient.

If naming the stages is a problem, you can simplify things by calling the stages the "fifth," "fourth," "third," and so on down to "first," arrival at which initiates the element.

Events within a given stage. In this step, you detail your list with each one of the events that compose a given stage, again from the most recent to the most remote. Don't try to describe the event, just find a name for it. Don't try to analyze, simply register the event. Continuing with my example:

	1.1.1. I write my list
	1.1.2. Brunch with a friend
1.1 THE RECAP.	1.1.3. Talking with a neighbor
LIST	1.1.4. Weekend in Cuernavaca
	1.1.5. Fixing the car
	1.1.6. I read about recapitulation

The number of events in each stage can vary greatly. A well-made list might have from 300 to 2000 events, or even more.

When your list is finished, it should form an enormous synoptic square of four columns: in the first, the name of the area; in the second, the elements of the area; in the third, the stages of the elements; in the fourth, the events that took place in each stage. The material can be organized as you choose (lists, numbered files, and so on). However, the synoptic square offers ease in making overall observations, which can be very revealing.

It is very important to finish one column before going on to the next; that is, the list is worked on in a vertical direction, not horizontal. This allows you to go over the components of your life repeatedly, each time with greater attention to detail. This will help you to become progressively more aware of the general direction of your life, to keep from getting lost when registering periods of your life that stand out particularly or are confusing to you. Ultimately, you should understand that, although the first columns help you to see your life from another perspective, only when you have finished the fourth will you be able to make maximum use of your list.

It must be emphasized that this list is an exercise in stalking, not based on analysis but on direct observation. The facts are simply registered without speculation or reflection. You also should avoid the tendency to leave out painful or shameful facts, which many times are the ones that demand a thorough recapitulation.

The time and attention you spend making your list will afford proportionately superior results. Generally, this will take two to twelve weeks minimum, working frequently. Having one area completed is usually enough to begin using the recapitulation box. A list with three areas well chosen and finished can be considered rather complete.

Although the list of events forms only one part of the technique of recapitulation, note that it can function very well by itself as a minimal form of general recapitulation. In my years of working with groups, I have observed the very noticeable effect that a well-made recapitulation list has on peoples' awareness and energy even without doing a full recapitulation inside the box. By simply making the list, the body can be made to remember. Once the list is finished, it becomes the "map" of your existence, by which you can observe its repetitions, periods, and sequences, and thereby reveal a great deal about the structural axes of your life.

10. BREATHING

Breathing is the magic element in the process of recapitulation, through which you can direct the repairs your body will have to make to its energetic structure. There are three types of breathing:

- Inhalation
- Exhalation
- The complete breath

A description of the first two is included in *The Eagle's Gift*. However, the description is not complete enough by itself for persons trying it on their own. It is done in the following manner:

Inhalation is the principal respiration in the exercise of recapitulation—respiration number one. Its central element, as its name indicates, is inhaling. It is the respiration that pulls, that attracts. It is used during two specific moments: when beginning a session of recapitulation inside the box; and when, during the session, we find an experience in which we lost energy, some experience that left us "incomplete."

The effects of this respiration permit the practitioner to pass from simple remembering to recapitulation proper, as well as to aid in the recovery of luminous fibers that have been left along the way.

To accomplish this, you must be relaxed in both body and mind. The spinal column must be straight, eyes closed. Begin by facing forward with the lungs empty. Without inhaling, turn your head until it faces over your right shoulder; starting from there, rotate 180 degrees until you are facing over the left shoulder, all the while taking in a deep slow breath until your lungs are completely filled with air. Both movement and breathing should be slow and synchronized. From the left shoulder, hold the air while turning to face forward, then slowly exhale, and you are back at the starting point. Make an almost imperceptible pause between each one of the movements.

This can be done whenever and as often as you feel is necessary, although generally a few minutes are enough.

Exhalation is the reverse of the first, and is called exhalation (or respiration) number two. Its central element is exhalation and its purpose is to separate or detach. It is used during recapitulation when we find an experience in which filaments from other people become attached to our own luminosity or when we encounter a "promise" we wish to be rid of.

Respiration number two liberates the body of foreign filaments and of "promises" that no longer need be honored. It is done in the same position and with the conditions indicated in number one, only in reverse. Begin by facing forward, inhaling slowly. Holding the air, turn to face over the left shoulder. Once there, slowly rotate your head 180 degrees while exhaling completely, until you are facing over the right shoulder. Lungs empty of air, you turn to face forward again to the starting position. Your body will tell you, through feeling, when to stop. Also the same slowness of movement, synchronization between breathing and movement, and pauses, are observed as in respiration number one.

The complete breath is used when we wish to clarify a scene from our past, to recover our sobriety, or simply when we want better concentration. Since this respiration forms part of other exercises, not only of recapitulation, a complete description of it will be found in chapter 6, exercise 46, on stopping the internal dialogue.

11. THE RECAPITULATION BOX

Fabrication. The box is a very powerful element in aiding recapitulation. It is both a tool and a symbol. As a tool it helps the body to remember. As a symbol it represents the limits of personal history in which we are held prisoners, the limits of the ego.

The recapitulation box, as its name implies, is a box, generally made of wood, which must be built while the person intending to use it is in a state of total concentration. Basically, it has the shape of a cube with one of its six sides fitted with hinges to function as a door. It need not form a perfect cube, but it must be constructed in such a way as to reduce the space around the body to no more than two inches at its closest approach. Its shape should permit the practitioner to enter, and sit down with the back straight and the legs crossed or drawn up against the chest to make the body as compact as possible. Allowance must also be made for adequate ventilation while at the same time reducing light entry to a minimum.

Other materials can be used, but wood is the best by virtue of the favorable influence that trees and tree products have on people.

A casket built by the user may be substituted in place of the box, in which case the practitioner would do the exercise lying down. Since it is naturally associated with death, a casket will facilitate recapitulation to a great extent. If there is a tendency to fall asleep, a small rock can be placed in such a way as to make things too uncomfortable for sleep.

It is best not to paint or draw designs on the box or to build it in a form other than the basic cube. Pyramids, for instance, besides provoking all sorts of metaphysical interpretations, produce a different effect, one that might well be disturbing. The use of metal parts (nails, hinges, etc.) should be reduced to a minimum. Any glue used should be organically based. Again, as with the list, the more time and concentration spent in fabricating the box, the more effective it will be in aiding us in our task.

Inside the box. Now that your list is ready (at least one area with all of its four columns finished), you are familiar with the three methods of breathing, and your box is constructed, you can go to work. Before entering the box, you must examine the most recent events on the list and memorize them in order to recall them once you are in the box.

Inside the box you will be concerned only with the fourth column from your list: the events. The number of events chosen should be no more than you consider possible to recapitulate in a single session. Theoretically, you should recapitulate one by one the events on the list beginning with the most recent and ending with the most remote. I say theoretically because in practice when the body recapitulates, it takes its own direction that often is not according to the order of the list. Sometimes events will appear that are not on the list and some you thought were very important pass to second place.

Once inside the box, begin practicing respiration number one for a few minutes. Each of you will have to determine for yourself the exact time required for this. The events will begin to arise by themselves; however, you can help by making a conscious effort to remember. There is no harm if you begin by using ordinary memory. In fact, the effort you put into making your list, the special breathing, and the box all combine to aid you in passing from ordinary memory to recapitulation. You can also try less obvious ways to remember. For example, focus your attention on more minor aspects of a given event instead of its central theme. If, for instance, the memory is about a discussion, what were some of the details in the room? What color were the walls? Try to remember the feelings that were present rather than the words that were spoken. Body sensations are very useful: What did I feel in my knees? How did my feet feel, my stomach? What odors were present? Once the process has begun, use the breathing exercises as necessary: one to recover energy, two to detach foreign filaments and to liberate yourself from promises and decisions no longer relevant to your life, and three to recover clarity and sobriety.

Once all the events on the list have been recapitulated, you must dispose of your box in a personal ritual that expresses the moment in which you have finally freed yourself from the confines of your personal history. The details of the ritual are strictly personal. The box should be burned or buried.

The total time needed for a complete recapitulation depends on many factors—life style, the intensity of the work, the length of sessions, their frequency, and so forth. In any case, you must take into account that time flows differently during recapitulation than it does in everyday life. If you consider that a dying person has time to do a complete recapitulation during the last moments of life, you can suppose that you also will not need years.

Recapitulation is best done during the hours when most people are asleep so as to be free of their extraneous thoughts. Also doing it in an unpopulated area will enhance the experience. Outdoors among trees is even better. Preferably, the box should be left in one place for the entire duration of the exercise. This lends an air of ritual to the experience. However, ideal conditions for recapitulation are not mandatory; the important thing is to do it, no matter where.

While some recapitulate for one or two hours, once or twice a week, others dedicate an entire weekend to it. It may take months to recapitulate the entire list. In workshops on recapitulation participants have worked for 21 days straight, recapitulating all night. Beginning with preliminary exercises at 7:30 pm, they enter the boxes an hour later and remain there until 5:30 am when everyone leaves to begin their daily activities. This is generally done in an unpopulated forested area near the city. Contrary to what you might expect, no one is worn out or tired after a night of this. In fact, the effect produced is one of vigor, not only in terms of energy, but also of consciousness and sobriety. The participants, as a result, begin to see their daily world from a more profound perspective.

It is not a problem, however, if you fall asleep inside the box. In no case will you simply be asleep—ordinary sleep, in fact, is not possible. The state which you enter into is beyond the dichotomy of simply being awake or asleep. Dreaming and recapitulation intermix in a reality that extends far beyond the limits of the box. You can also expect strange effects inside the box—noises, voices, images, or find yourself awake in a reality not that of the box. All of this is normal. Whatever happens, you can be sure that your trip will be to there and back again. *In no case should anyone else be allowed inside your box, since it becomes charged with your vibrations and such an intrusion could cause fright or illness to the intruder.*

While recapitulating, let your feelings flow freely. If you are in a place where you cannot cry, yell, or laugh, it would be better to look for a more isolated place.

Also, you should avoid calling excessive attention to your box and/or the exercise, especially to those who are totally unprepared to understand what these exercises are all about. If someone should ask about it, simply say that it is "my meditation box" or some such thing. Any attention from outsiders about your work can create obstacles for you.

This is the end of that which relates to recapitulation.

THE PETTY TYRANT

This technique, combining both pragmatism and humor, is one of the most refined of the art of stalking. In its most general form, it can be applied to any situation in which we find ourselves subjected to adverse circumstances against our will, especially those in which our personal ego is affected. These would be situations involving offense, humiliation, or mistreatment.

As presented to us by Castaneda, the technique of the petty tyrant represents one of the finest points of stalking. It was developed during the period of the Spanish conquest of Mexico, in which sorcerers and men of knowledge were subjected to tremendous pressure under the yoke of the Spaniards. The majority of sorcerers were killed; but some made use of the situation, out of which grew the art of stalking, thanks to which the survivors were able to come out ahead under the most adverse of circumstances. In developing their art, they made use of the persecution, domination, and mistreatment they received. This taught them how to move about undetected and handle situations in such a way that—if they were not killed—they emerged in the end victorious. They converted their dealings with petty tyrants into a matter of strategy. But their most important discovery was that in dealing strategically with petty tyrants, they encountered a very effective remedy for self-importance. Since that is the most energy-consuming activity in the life of an individual, its eradication became one of the prime objectives for stalkers interested in using that energy to enter into the unknown.

Don Juan gives a very simple definition of the petty tyrant in *The Fire From Within*: "A petty tyrant is a tormentor, someone who holds the power of life or death over warriors or simply annoys them to distraction . . ." (VII-31). The stalkers of the colonial era classified petty tyrants in categories according to their level of influence. Far above the human level was put the inexorable force that sustains all that exists, the primary energy of the entire universe, and they called it simply "The Tyrant". Compared to this force, the most powerful and cruel of men were no more than petty tyrants; those were put at the top of the list.

- *Petty tyrants*—have the power of life and death over their victims according to whim.
- *Little petty tyrants*—harass and can inflict injury without killing their victims.
- *Small-fry petty tyrants*—are bothersome and exasperating to no end.

Naturally, during the Spanish conquest there were petty tyrants present everywhere. However, the warriors who came later and those of today generally have to make do with little petty tyrants; they were divided into four categories:

- Those who torment with brutality and violence.
- Those who create unbearable apprehension.
- Those who oppress with sadness and gloom.
- Those who torment by making people rage.

As related in *The Fire From Within*, in dealing with petty tyrants, stalkers rely on the first four elements of the stalker's strategy which we will look at now.

12. THE STALKER'S STRATEGY

These six elements have a reciprocal influence on each other. The first five have to do with a warrior's private world and are called "the attributes of warriorship" (VII-31). The sixth is an element belonging to the outside world. Each element, except for the fifth, is part of the world of the known.

- *Control*—to tune the spirit when the petty tyrant is trampling on you.

- *Discipline*—to gather information on the petty tyrant while he is beating you up.

- *Forbearance*—to wait patiently, without haste or anxiety; a simple joyful holding back of the payment due.

- *Timing*—to put in action everything that was prepared by control, discipline, and forbearance. Timing opens the gate of the dam.

- *Will*—the only element belonging to the realm of the unknown.

- *The petty tyrant*—a tormentor who makes life impossible. Warriors use him or her to eliminate their own self-importance and to learn impeccability.

To use this technique requires a degree of work experience and awareness not apt to be found among beginners. You must maintain a minimum level of sobriety to uphold a strategy in situations where ordinary people are too preoccupied with emotional outbursts to be able to look at the situation from a different perspective.

Commentary on the technique

Any encounter with a petty tyrant, even a very small one is damaging and offensive for ordinary people. However, what really finishes us off is not so much any real damage inflicted but a feeling of offense and humiliation that arises from taking ourselves too seriously. If we examine the petty tyrants in our lives, we should ask what damage they really cause us. A sober observation will reveal that the real enemy is within ourselves. It is our self-importance that is poking us

inside when we find ourselves in a situation that is disagreeable to the ego. A warrior could suffer physical damage but
would in no way be offended by the actions of a petty tyrant.
A warrior could be struck physically but would not feel
humiliated. This extra energy not spent on self-importance is
precisely the advantage the warrior has over the petty tyrant,
whose principal characteristic—and weak point—is taking
himself or herself with deadly seriousness. With this extra
energy a warrior maintains strategy, control, and the ability
to observe, then places traps and waits. The warrior triumphs
in the end, having achieved the tempering of his or her spirit.

An attitude like that—being attentive, taking each situation as a challenge, and dealing with it strategically—is useful not only in confrontations with petty tyrants but for any
situation where we may feel attacked, humiliated, or offended. How many new possibilities are waiting for us if we do
not react from our self-importance? The answer can be found
only through practice.

A person not preoccupied with the mental torture of
being offended will be in a better position to avoid any kind
of damage. Remember the situation of the man pursued by a
lion: he has to run. If he wastes time becoming angry with
the lion or feels offended by the "abuse" received from the
animal, he will be lost. In a like manner, in interaction among
humans, our self-importance makes us incapable of acting at
just the right moment; consequently the results are always
predictable.

One last word in regard to this technique. It should be
used with caution. *One must remember that a petty tyrant is an
enemy.* I mention this because there is always someone who
says, "Ah, what luck! I already have my petty tyrant at home
. . . it's my wife (or husband). Be careful with this kind of friv-
olousness because that situation probably requires honesty
and compassion instead of confrontation, even were it done
strategically. It must also be remembered that since the attitude of the stalker—not giving in to self-importance—is

applicable in any and all circumstances, the petty tyrant must be in a position of power in relation to the stalker, an external factor normally not under our control. We cannot label someone a "petty tyrant" simply because we don't like him or her.

13. INTENDING APPEARANCES

Working with appearances is another technique of stalking, one that can be as fun as it can be devastating. It has to do with artistic creation in the most authentic sense. It deals to a certain extent with the art of the actor as well as the art of disguise.

The principal characteristic of this technique, in which you disguise yourself and/or act like someone completely different from your everyday self, is not only to convince the spectators but also to convince yourself to such a degree that the force of your conviction is transmitted to the spectators. This is a modification of perception, a movement of the assemblage point.

Carried to its extreme, the art of pure acting is the art of the sorcerer and the nagual—the art of transformation. What do sorcerers experience when converting into crows and flying away? In principle they feel as though they fly, feel themselves crows, seeing and experiencing the world as such. Their secret is that they are capable of modifying their perceptions to match that of a crow, modifying the position of their assemblage point. Their knowledge of sorcery, their conviction, and their years of work allow them to achieve it. But now we have a question, one that Castaneda put to don Juan long ago: What would a spectator see? An average spectator would probably just see a sleeping person and might think him or her drunk or intoxicated. But a spectator in a state of nonordinary awareness or one observing a sorcerer of extraordinary power—one who could force, with the power of his conviction, the movement of the spectator's assemblage point—surely would see a miracle: a person transformed into a crow and flying away. And Castaneda asks the question again: Was that real what I felt? To which don Juan replies: "There is no reality other than that which you felt . . . reality is a feeling."

In the case of true acting, something similar occurs but to a somewhat lesser extent. Unless of course the actor happens to be a man of knowledge whose particular art is acting, like the nagual Julian in *The Power of Silence*. In such a case, what happens is exactly the same.

Whoever has experienced a theatrical representation of true art has witnessed this magic. Ordinary reality disappears; now there is no theater, no actors, no spectators. We have penetrated into an alternate reality thanks to the magic of the actors. They have penetrated this other reality and taken us along with them. They have left behind not only the everyday world but also their former egos, thereby transforming themselves into entirely new characters, who now become real.

In the many workshops on stalking I have conducted, we have practiced theater under many diverse conditions—from street theater to secret theater—in which the spectators become as involved as the actors without realizing it, taking it for reality. Our work ranges from the art of mimicry to the representation of works in indigenous communities where Spanish is not spoken.

I have discovered, among other things, that true acting functions as a doorway to the other self, to the experience outside the ego—a quality which by itself would make this a practice worthy of exploration. When you convert yourself into your personage, when you are capable of moving your perception to become its living expression, your former ego is revealed in its true dimensions. And your old life as well. You realize that the ego, and the world in which you once believed you were trapped, was only a mirage, just one more character in one more play, with actors who had forgotten they were acting on a stage. This is significant especially when the play you portray is one of pain or boredom.

14. ACTOR FOR A FEW DAYS

This technique can help a great deal to diminish self-importance, to erase personal history, and to view your everyday life from another perspective. It consists of the following steps:

1. First you must choose or create a character with very well-defined traits—preferably one with characteristics diametrically opposed to your own.

2. Take time to study the character thoroughly in order to know all details. You have to determine how he or she talks, thinks, feels, dresses, moves, and so forth.

3. Next, prepare your character's entry into the world. Obtain the proper clothing, and begin practicing personal manifestations in private—attitudes, vocabulary, interests, activities.

4. Go public and interact disguised as your character. You must remain active, go out, converse, visit places, work—according to the role you are playing. It requires a minimum of discipline in order not to slip back into your everyday self. The key is to convince yourself of the role, feel it intimately, and think as the character would—make it a real person.

15. DISGUISES

The idea here is to disguise yourself so well that no one is able to recognize you. This of course depends not only on a good disguise, but on a good characterization as well. Attitudes, tone of voice, and so forth, must all be congruent with the disguise. This should be done so well that not even family members could recognize you. The procedure for this is:

1. Obtain the disguise.

2. Put it on and practice the characterization.

3. Disguised, observe the space in which your ordinary life takes place for a period of at least one day.

4. Disguised, interact in that space with the people who know you, but without giving yourself away.

This exercise allows you to observe your everyday world, your relationships, the people closest to you, from an unusual perspective. Naturally, your disguise must be effective and appropriate for interacting among the people who know you, who, of course, will consider you a stranger. Play the role of a salesman of religious books, a survey taker, a beggar, or a fireman—any of these would work. Thus disguised, go to your house, your work, to school, and speak with family members, friends, and acquaintances. The more prolonged your interaction and the more areas of your life you observe, the greater will be your results.

This exercise may be practiced as often and as long as you like, but at a minimum it should be at least one whole day. Also it can be changed periodically; you can change your disguise on different occasions, or go into more depth with the original character. With this exercise, you must be prepared for surprises where they are least expected.

16. DISGUISED AS A MEMBER OF THE OPPOSITE SEX

This is a variation of the preceding exercise that deserves separate mention due to its singular effect. In *The Power of Silence*, don Juan tells us that ". . . only in a woman's disguise can any man really learn the art of stalking" (VIII-88). It also serves as an excellent way to train yourself in the four moods of stalking, which have already been discussed.

The exercise consists of disguising yourself (a man) as a woman so well as to be totally convincing to any observer. Acting as a woman, you must be ruthless, cunning, patient, and sweet, which are often qualities natural to a woman. Since a woman's universe is totally foreign to a man, it is recommended that you practice it thoroughly in order to "have an inkling of what being a woman is like" (VIII-88).

As a woman practicing this exercise, you would, in a similar manner, disguise yourself as a man and act as such. This would involve discovering and emulating facets of the masculine universe such as: mental steadfastness, competitiveness, concern over social recognition, and so on.

It should be mentioned that this technique will lose much of its effectiveness if done in a "less involving" environment such as among your friends. In order for this exercise to have value, it must be done among strangers who, thanks to your disguise, will really think they are dealing with a woman—in the case of a male stalker—or with a man in the case of a female one. This exercise is one that almost invariably will cause the assemblage point to move.

17. OBSERVING TONALS

The way this exercise is presented in *Tales of Power* (IV-137) probably seems too fantastic to some readers. If they cannot see persons as "luminous eggs", perhaps the practice seems inaccessible to them. There exists, however, a simplified version for beginners that can give very positive results.

Begin by choosing a point from which you can discreetly observe a large number of people going about their daily routines—a subway station, a park, a street, any place where people are found in large numbers. As a beginning stalker you should be relaxed and simply observe people, avoiding judgments or speculations about how someone looks or acts; instead try to sense each person you observe. Stopping the internal dialogue, while not indispensable, is nonetheless highly desirable. Repeating the word *nothing, nothing, nothing,* over and over in your mind will tend to keep out any extraneous thoughts. Your main task here is to concentrate on what you sense from each person.

Among other things, you should perceive if the observed person has "a good tonal" or not. In more mundane terms, it means whether or not the person has a good life, takes care of himself or herself, is strong and happy. You will be lucky indeed if you can find someone like that.

If someone appears with the indicated characteristics, try to speak to that person and establish a conversation without revealing the true nature of what you are doing. Your attitude should be natural, avoiding any impulse to "corner" such a person or to try to establish a relationship unless conditions are favorable for such—and then only if you feel the course of the whole affair is congruent with the nature of your work. Your main concern is merely to corroborate your perception by interacting, all the while remaining alert in order to respond appropriately to whatever the situation may demand of you.

You will have to see just how many healthy people you can find.

FIVE

THE NOT-DOINGS OF THE PERSONAL SELF

DESTRUCTURING THE EGO

Not-doing in general is the basic strategy a sorcerer uses to enter into the separate reality and under which—ultimately—are grouped the different techniques such as stalking and *dreaming*. The not-doings of the personal self constitute a specialized area within the totality of the techniques known as stalking. These techniques are understood to be practices specifically designed to destructure the warrior's ego as well as his or her ordinary view of the world—two phenomena that, as we already know, are reciprocal.

While all the techniques in general tend to produce the same result, this particular group of exercises has an immediate and direct effect on the living experience of the self, in how you experience yourself.

In *Journey to Ixtlan* (which in my opinion is one of his most direct and accessible works in terms of practical application), Castaneda describes three principal forms of not-doings of the personal self: using death as an adviser, losing self-importance, and erasing personal history, which is broken down into separate techniques. All of these tend to produce what we would call in anti-psychiatry the destructuring of the ego.[9] Such destructuring represents a doorway to freedom for a warrior who has worked to achieve it and, at the same time, a doorway to insanity for an average person who may undergo such changes accidentally through an intense emotional crisis.

SLAVES OF A DESCRIPTION

When I say "ego", I mean all that is referred to when we say the word "I". Just what exactly is this "I"? I don't really know, but it feels as though it is located in my head, behind my eyes. And what about the body? I feel that the body is not "I" but something that "I" possess for my use; that is, for transport, for showing off to others, and so forth. That's why it is referred to as "my" body. And what about energy? For example, what about the field of energy that is my being and extends beyond the limits of my skin? No one speaks of that. As average people we do not as a rule even conceive of such a thing, to say nothing of considering this field as part of "I".

If the ego is not my body or my energy, then what is it? What is it made of? The absurd but true answer is: nothing. If someone doubts this, then let that person try to search for it. If we dissect the human body we will find things such as heart, lungs, veins, blood, glands, brain, among many others. But we will find no ego. In fact, no ego is found either in the body of the newly born or in one who has died.

To this, a reasonable, normal person might well respond: "But this can't be! The ego is nothing? I am nothing? That means I don't exist? Of course I exist!" (What is upset here is the ego and not the totality of the person.)

---

[9] See David Cooper, *La Muerte de la Familia*, Barcelona: Ariel, 1985.

The response of a reasonable but not so normal person might be: "Very well, I suppose you exist. But if you are an 'I' (ego) and when you say 'I', you're not referring to your body, then to what are you referring? What are you? Who are you that makes you call yourself 'I'? What are you made of?"

Here are some typical answers from a normal person:

- Well, I, in reality, how should I tell you?...ah!, I know!
- I am a sincere person.
- I am the son of my mother.
- I am a good husband.
- I am lazy.
- I am afraid of women.
- I am bla, bla, bla.
- I am etc., etc., etc.

Correct. The ego is all those things. The ego is that description. (Do exercise 22, Ego: the verbal portrait.)

Precisely. The ego is a description. Nothing else. Words, just words. It has no specific reality. What's more, the ego is a specific mass of nothing, whose quasi reality arises from our insistence that we behave as though it were real.

The truth is that human beings are not what is contained in the description of their ego, although they believe that to be the case, by virtue of which they behave in accordance with the description. This is manifested through their routines, which are the active expression of the content of the description that we call the ego.

This can be proved only through the practice of the not-doings of the personal self. In the "doings" of everyday life, we are like this or like that. We are capable of some things but not others. Nevertheless, in practicing not-doing, practitioners discover that they are capable of doing many things that were formerly regarded as impossible because they were not contained in the description, and that, certainly, is good news.

ACTING PURPOSEFULLY

We can act outside the description. Essentially anyone engaged in an act not in agreement with the content of the description that calls itself "I" is performing a "not-doing of the personal self". This is indeed possible to carry out. I have proven it in myself and in the work groups. There was no power of suggestion involved here, nor did I imagine it. It is real.

We have all been educated to believe that the ego is our only reality, to believe that that is who we are and will be until the end. We have forgotten we weren't always that way. We have forgotten that once we were "without form", which permitted us to be amazed, to feel everything and everyone as a discovery, as a mystery. We have forgotten the mystery of ourselves and of the world because we trained ourselves to believe that we were something defined with definite boundaries (the ego). We did the same with everyone and everything else around us, giving force to the spell of black magic that constitutes the life of modern people: to reduce the inconceivable, the mysterious, and the miracle of being alive to just so much nonsense. And boring nonsense at that. We put ourselves in prison and we call it "I". How marvelous! Here we have a man or woman with "personality".

But I have news for you. We are not condemned to live forever trapped inside a description. We can destructure ourselves. We can erase our personal history. We can regain our freedom.

PSYCHOTIC DESTRUCTURATION

The phenomenon of psychotic madness deserves a brief commentary. Psychosis has to do with the violent destructuring of reality and the ego. Not that psychotics "hallucinate" things that do not exist. Rather, they are perceiving things that exist, but they organize them psychically and emotionally in a way that is different from the ordinary. Or they perceive things that normal people discard unconsciously, which results in the perception of a reality that for psychotics is generally painful and many times self-destructive. This destructuring they experience as a loss of certainty as to what is real, including the ego itself, which has lost its sense of continuity due to the "disassembling" of its reality. At this point psychotics will have serious doubts about their identity since they are no longer certain about what were the original characteristics of their ego. Since the ego forms the fundamental basis of conduct, its destructuring is what causes the psychotic to appear erratic and incoherent.

Unless the insanity has to do with a tumor or genetic defects, an insane person is really one who entered into an uncontrolled process of destructuring the ego, although not aware of it, and he or she entered it with motivations similar to those of the warrior. It is a search for an alternative way of being, a rejection of sick normality, whose price is boredom and anguish when it's not pain and depression. The psychotic is in a desperate search for freedom, a condition originally due to some great personal, unhealed existential crisis. We could say that he or she "fell by the wayside".

But that psychotic path does lead somewhere. It leads to freedom from an oppressive existence. The problem for the psychotic person is the lack of power to arrive at the destination of freedom.[10]

THE DESTRUCTURATION OF THE WARRIOR

The path that warriors take to freedom can also make them crazy, but they do it without losing themselves. This is what don Juan meant by "controlled folly" in *A Separate Reality*. And while psychotics are immersed in madness not of their own choosing and beyond their ability to control, warriors go about the process of destructuring the ego harmoniously. Their normality disappears at the same time their

---

[10] Anti-psychiatrists have studied psychotics to the point where they can speak with some authority on the subject. (See David Cooper, *Psiquiatría y Antipsiquiatría*, Barcelona: Paidós, 1985.)

energy, control, and sobriety are increasing. They know the "way of the warrior" and, putting all their trust in it, they use it to move about in a world of amazement and mystery. A world of challenges and battles, of creation. And from their controlled destiny, warriors are capable of moving about in the most appropriate way with the rest of society, so much so that they are considered "most reasonable people."

If we observe that we were not born with an ego, but as adults we possess one, then logically we must have picked it up somewhere along the way. We were compelled to create one beginning from infancy, finishing with it by the time we reached adulthood. However, since we were the ones who did the work of forming our ego, we possess the possibility of erasing it and creating another one in its place—one created by us, created intentionally. From this point of view, stalking could well be considered the art of reinventing the self. As a result of not-doings, stalkers are not slaves to one way of being. They instead are able to create new ways of being to fit new situations, transforming themselves any time circumstances require it or just for their own curiosity.

INTRODUCTION FOR EXERCISES RELATING TO THE AWARENESS OF DEATH

In so-called modern societies, one of the central "doings" on which is built the ego of the individual—and by extension the "ego" of the society—is the denial of death.

We are trained very young to forget the fact that we are going to die. This forgetting naturally alleviates part of our fear of the unknown but at the same time charges the very high price of making us forget the magical nature of life.

This widespread denial of death is prevalent in European and European-based cultures. But it is not in any way universal. Knowledge of death was one of the basic values that governed people's lives on a social as well as individual level in the pre-Columbian cultures of the American continent, particularly the ancient Toltecs.

The custom in first world cultures to buy "life insurance," to pay for our own burial on credit, to inherit property, and the violent shock produced when we witness another person's death, are some examples of just how far we have been trained to consider ourselves immortal. Religions selling all sorts of different heavens and resurrections through which we have to ascend after death play a fundamental role in conspiring to help us forget that we are mortal. Although this phenomenon is not exclusively Western, it is here, using the logic of consumerism, where the role it plays in denying the reality of death is most efficient and emphatic. Making donations to the church—basically a consumer act—is, for example, more or less unconsciously one way to buy ourselves a "little bit of heaven." We can see that when certain aspects of Oriental religions like Hinduism, such as yoga, penetrate into our Western world, we find certain elements such as reincarnation, very attractive. Other more subtle aspects such as inner silence or the practice of leading a simple life go almost unnoticed.

We are prepared to pay almost any price in order to keep on believing we are immortal.

It seems strange we were taught to forget the one inevitable event in our lives: the fact of our death. Death represents the mysterious. It is the unknown. And we have been taught to fear the mysterious and the unknown.

At the bottom it is the ego who fears death and rightly so. Faced with it, the ego is reduced to what it really is: nothing. *Death is not the negation of life, but rather the negation of the ego. Life, on the other hand, is sustained by death.* The life of our bodies is nourished by the deaths of animals and plants, just as our bodies will serve as nourishment for them upon our own death. Thus, inasmuch as the ego and death are antithetical to one another, the awareness of death represents one way to carry us—alive—beyond the boundaries of the ego.

While the ego has no way of dealing with death, our body, as a field of energy, has intrinsic knowledge of its true destiny. Our other self can deal directly with the mysterious and interact with the unknown without interference from the noncomprehension of the rational mind. Thus, the awareness of death is a doorway to the awareness of being: we are luminous beings. We are fields of energy, not egos.

Awareness of this can only be found outside the world of words. As in recapitulation, we are dealing here with body memory nearer to feeling than to reason.

If immortality forms one of the basic structural "doings" of the average person, then the corresponding "not-doing"—awareness of death—forms one of the fundamental techniques in the way of the warrior.

And upon the doings of immortality rest the majority of the most energy-consuming doings of the ego and its routines. Self-importance, for instance, is possible only if we feel immortal. Our most common doings are revealed as monstrous when seen in the light of our mortality. Because we feel immortal we permit ourselves:

- To postpone, for a nonexistent tomorrow, things that we can only do today.

- To repress affection, denying its expression, forgetting that the only time to touch, caress, or come together is today, a time that will be brief in any event.

- To ignore beauty and learn instead to see everything as "ugly." (Let us imagine the beauty of a flower for the person who is no longer able to appreciate it.)

- To defend the image we have of ourselves.

- To indulge ourselves in feelings of hate, rancor, offense, and pettiness.

- To worry about things to the point of depression and anguish.

- To complain, to feel impatient or defeated.

Conscious mortals would not allow themselves to waste their only time, brief and irreplaceable, with such defeating emotions. Therefore conscious mortals are warriors who make each act into a challenge: the challenge to savor the marrow of life in each instant. The challenge to live each moment with dignity, as impeccably as their power permits them. Mortals enjoy the value of each precious moment because they know with total certainty that death is stalking them, that their appointment with it will have to be kept without fail. Since death can touch them at any moment, warriors give themselves to it beforehand, considering each act their last act on Earth (III-101). Therefore, they give the best of themselves.

Naturally, the acts of beings who—in light of inevitable death—are giving the best of themselves would have special power. Their acts have force and flavor that cannot be compared to the boring repetitions of an immortal. Warriors make the awareness of inevitable death their cornerstone of knowledge and of struggle. Instead of believing in empty values and abstract ideas that would give them false ideas about their destiny, they rest their knowledge on the one sure event in life: death.

As was mentioned before, arriving at the awareness of inevitable death is not a matter of reflection. It is not a mental concept but rather a phenomenon of body consciousness. The awareness of death lies in left-side consciousness; it is one of the aspects of awareness of the other self, and only through the practice of "not-doing" can it be recovered.

Using death as an adviser is a form of not-doing that can be used to rescue this awareness, while giving us the opportunity to deal with matters of daily life from a much more sober, efficient, and realistic perspective than an average person.

TECHNIQUES

The not-doings of the personal self are organized into three basic techniques (awareness of death, erasing personal history, and eliminating self-importance) from which can be derived many practical applications. Here are the basic techniques as well as some concrete examples.

18. DEATH AS AN ADVISER (III-43)

When you feel worn out by life, or are about to crumble, remember your death. Take a few moments outside the dynamics of daily events to assess the reality of the situation, and to measure it against the fact of your inevitable death.

This is especially useful in moments when self-importance is indulging in one of its many variants, gaining control of your person and your moment: you feel self-pity; you feel you are losing something very valuable; you are offended or feel a desire for revenge; you are tied to something that, in reality, you have already lost; you are mean and deny love; you are fearful; you fear to act according to your deepest wishes. These are the moments in which to take a look into the dark eyes of death and ask its advice. You need the control necessary to look at matters in light of your death—who waits for you—and consider the situation as though it were your last act before dying. Until death eliminates all pettiness and fear. Until death puts everything in its place, in its proper perspective. Only then can you see that alongside death, the most weighty of everyday problems pales in comparison. You are alive; and death waits for you. That is the only thing that matters. The rest are just trifles.

INTRODUCTION FOR EXERCISES RELATING TO THE AWARENESS OF THE SKELETON

Exercises practiced in our work groups that have proven very useful in reaching the awareness of death are those exercises called the awareness of the skeleton. They were born of an inspiration by one of the coordinators who worked with us, the musician German Bringas, after he had read "The Skeleton" by Ray Bradbury. It occurred to Bringas that here were ideas for the formation of new exercises. Practicing them, we have discovered their force, and we continue to work with them, creating new exercises. Following are some of the forms in which we have practiced them.

19. AWAKENING THE SKELETON
These are to be done at night, in a group or individually.

1. Find a fairly large open area, out of doors. If done in a group, someone will need to direct the exercise.

2. Everyone should stand completely immobile and relaxed.

3. Then, almost imperceptibly at first, begin moving. Start with small movements in one finger. Gradually pass to the other fingers, the hand, the arms, and so on until the entire body is moving in slow motion. Try to be physically conscious of the body in each movement.

4. Begin to do movements similar to a sit up, but from a standing position. Move slowly at first, picking up speed very gradually, almost imperceptibly. Breathe in coordination with movement, your attention on the physical sensations of the body. Increase speed until, after about 15 minutes, maximum velocity and effort are reached. Look for a moment of true catharsis as you near the peak of maximum effort.

5. Reaching catharsis, let out a powerful scream, which gives emphasis to the feeling being experienced, all the while remaining in conscious contact with the body.

6. After the scream, begin to reduce speed, again almost imperceptibly. At this point, bodily awareness should be very apparent. Direct that awareness toward sensing the bones of the entire body. You should feel as if you were nothing but bones. In this state, gradually reduce movements until you are completely immobile once again.

7. Slowly lower yourself down into a squatting position, arms between your legs, hands on the ground in a simian position.

8. Now begin to deepen the awareness of your skeleton, visualizing a skeleton in a squatting position. Your head should feel like a skull. You are a being made of white

stone. As a skeleton, you are a mysterious being looking at the world with curiosity and amazement. Breathe deeply. Imagine your eyes to be two dark holes looking into infinity. Remain in the squatting position until the sensation of the skeleton is very clear.

9. Fully aware of the skeleton, begin to move very slowly. Stand up first and then begin to move. Take three steps forward, three steps back. Try to see the world as a skeleton would. Perceive the others in the group as skeletons.

20. TOUCHING THE SKELETON

This exercise is done in pairs. Following all the steps outlined above, the partners face each other and, with eyes closed, you begin to touch the bone structure of your partner who remains immobile. Try to sense, through touch, the shape and sensation of the skull and the rest of the bones. Smoothly and softly, with curiosity, touch the ridges around the eyes, nose, cranium, teeth, roof of mouth, collarbone, scapula, ribs, and so forth. Using tactile sense, try to "visualize" the skeleton in front of you. As the person touching, imagine yourself as one skeleton touching another; the person receiving concentrates on deepening the awareness of his or her own skeleton. Take approximately 20 minutes for this exercise.

21. THE DANCE OF THE SKELETON

This exercise is best done with appropriate background music, preferably without words and of a type that invites concentration and sensitivity, music that conveys a feeling of mystery and beauty.

This is a variation of the two preceding exercises in which after having followed all the indicated steps, including the touching of both partners' skeletons, the music begins and the pair of skeletons begins to dance. Dance in free form using movement to express your feelings of being alive as skeletons in the world. The magic that allows your skeleton to stand upright represents the brief magic of life. This magic endows the white stone with life, and when it is withdrawn, the stone again becomes inert. The skeletons dance to this magic and to the shadows among which they move. This will take 10 to 20 minutes.

Commentary on the techniques

These exercises are to be done in darkness. Practice in an uninhabited area such as a forest, desert, or an open field for best results. The bottom of a canyon or a dry riverbed is excellent. It is easier to do during a full moon. Places near the ocean should be avoided, however. Also, someone should coordinate the exercises, initiate their different phases, start the music, and verbalize helpful phrases for the participants. Naturally, the presence of strangers and interruptions are to be avoided.

INTRODUCTION FOR EXERCISES RELATING TO ERASING PERSONAL HISTORY

Erasing personal history is perhaps the most general of the not-doings of the personal self, since, in one way or other, it encompasses all the techniques of not-doing. It assumes the termination of the cause/effect relationship between the past and the present.

Don Juan suggests to Carlos that he erase his personal history (III-26). He refers not only to Carlos's need to change his way of being and living, but also to the possibility that such change would, in effect, break the determination of his past, what the sorcerer called his "personal history".

This idea seems strange to us not only because we are accustomed to think of the past as forming the foundation of the present, but also because we tend to regard the past as something unchangeable, which of course gives us a perfect excuse not to change. In working with groups, I continue to be amazed as people affirm time and time again that they want to change while at the same time they do everything possible to remain the same. Most of the time, they justify the past. "It's that I never learned to discipline myself." "It's that I have always been weak." "It's that I was over-protected by my parents." It's that, it's that. . . . And the "it's that" always has to do with the past.

Erasing personal history is a magical possibility that is difficult to explain using rational logic. Erase the past—don't try to overcome it, simply erase it. This does not imply that we can erase past events from our lives. Rather it is the breaking of the relationships we have established with them, whose most common modes of expression are in our way of being and the way in which we live.

If personal history is the principal obstacle to change, then the power to erase it represents the doorway to freedom.

Resistance to behaving in novel ways arises from the belief that we are incapable of doing anything outside the inventory of past actions. We resist change. And when we try to change, we find personal history to be the major obstacle standing in our way. Family and friends also tend to resist our change; being so familiar with our personal history, they do not allow us to act outside its dictates. The encounter with the unknown poses the problem of not knowing how to behave with something for which they lack the proper training, and therefore they avoid it.

I remember a rather dramatic example of this: Several years ago, I had in a workshop a 19-year-old woman with a life full of problems—drug addiction, alcoholism, unemployment, poor family communication, and so on. I found her submerged in suicidal depression and very weak from her self-destructive habits. With time and work she managed to overcome her problems. She fought for change, gave up alcohol and drugs, got a job, and little by little her energy was restored. However, as a result of these changes, her problems at home began to increase. The fighting at home became more severe. On one occasion, she told of an argument she had with her older brother, who scolded her for behaving so strangely. The family didn't know where she spent her time, who her new friends were, or the reason for her sudden change. They were so habituated to consider her "incorrigible" that this unlooked-for and mysterious change caused them great uneasiness. They could not forgive her. Her brother said, "What's happening to you? You've gone crazy and I can't understand you! You were better before; we prefer you as an alcoholic and drug addict than as a crazy person." In the end, she opted for her independence and followed her own course.

The struggle to erase personal history is a fight not only against certain internalized elements of our being—that can give security by maintaining the ego in a reality that, pleasant or not, is at least familiar—but also against a history that has been internalized by those who are close to us and to whom it gives security as well. There is nothing more menacing to the ego than dealing with a person whom we cannot classify. Personal history gives us several labels with which we define our own person, reducing ourselves to just a few characteristics. Likewise, we classify everyone around us using similar labels that we derive from their personal history, real or imaginary. Since we can't deal with the mysterious, we prefer to deal with labels. Therefore no one surprises us. We are more sure of ourselves the more quickly we can classify people.

Don Juan advises Carlos that if he wishes to be free from the ties of what other people think about him, he must begin to erase himself, creating a fog around him that would make him into a mysterious and unpredictable being. This strategy is not only directed toward the outside world. We must erase ourselves to the point where we also become a mystery even to ourselves. The third precept of stalkers is considering themselves also a mystery, along with the other mysteries of the world.

The loss of certainty as to whom we suppose ourselves to be, which emanates from personal history, is congruent and reciprocal with the loss of certainty as to what we normally consider to be the real world. Again we find that the reality of the ego and external reality as well are nothing more than descriptions. Thus, the process of erasing applies not only to personal history but also to our ordinary description of the world.

The battlefield that lies beyond the description is the field of the unknown, the field where nothing is written down beforehand; it is not the self or the world. It is the place where we can create, choose, or be anything we want to be. It is the field of freedom.

22. EGO: A VERBAL PORTRAIT

This technique is an individual exercise that is useful for yourself, and it also functions very well as a preparation for different types of not-doings of the personal self, such as the individualized not-doings. It consists of a written portrait, as faithful as possible, of your own person and your way of life but in the third person as though you were dealing with someone else. It should contain the following:

- Name
- Age
- Physical characteristics
- Manner of dress
- Way of being
- State of health
- Places frequented
- Places avoided
- Most common moods
- Type of people attracted to
- Type of people avoided
- Types of work done in the past, and current work
- Characteristics of emotional life
- Kind of image projected to the world
- Daily routines
- Internal structural routines (cyclical repetitions)
- Manner of speaking
- Conversational themes

- Ways in which free time is spent
- Way in which sexuality is approached
- Economic situation
- Major virtues
- Major defects
- The best things done
- The worst things done
- The best things that have happened
- The worst things that have happened

Commentary on the technique

It is very important to make the description in the third person and to do it as coldly and factually as possible, with total indifference, as though we were dealing with someone we were neither for nor against. If done conscientiously, we will very easily obtain a description of our ego; and without a doubt that ego is nothing more than a description, which we cultivate through our actions. The moment we immerse ourselves in the practice of not-doing, what we normally know as "I" is revealed in its true dimensions: a description—like the one written down on paper—that can be modified or simply thrown away.

23. BEGINNING TO ERASE YOURSELF

Don Juan's first instructions regarding the erasing of personal history (III-31) can serve as beginning exercises for all people interested in freeing themselves from the confines of their personal history:

1. Don't automatically reveal everything you do to other people around you, since this impulse comes from the ego's desire to confirm itself, thus fortifying personal history.

2. Begin by dealing not only with those people you know well but also interact with people who have not classified you in agreement with a common past.

3. Avoid having to explain and justify everything that you do and tactfully refuse anyone who demands an explanation.

4. Don't reveal to anyone what you are up to. It does no good to hide if everyone knows you are hiding.

24. TELLING YOURSELF LIES (III-213)

This technique of consciously lying to the self as a form of not-doing has proven itself very effective especially for liberating the self from self-degrading aspects of personal history—those that picture a "horrible" image. I have recommended it in particular to people who manifest a high level of self-deprecation, thinking that they are the worst people alive.

1. Begin by making an inventory of your thoughts (as in the stalking procedure for determining energy expenditures, exercise number 1) for a period of eight days. If you are in some kind of crisis of self-degradation, however, three days will be sufficient.

2. Opposite your most characteristic negative thoughts, write the complements such as:

TRUTH	LIES
I am envious	It makes me glad to see other people happy
I have no willpower	I complete everything I start
I repress my feelings	I am free to express what I feel
I am ugly and unattractive	I am truly attractive
I have failed my family	I have fulfilled my family's expectation of me
I am afraid to fail	I feel sure I will succeed

3. During a period of one to three weeks (depending on the severity of the case), repeat these lies to yourself as often as possible. Think them as though they were the truth. Should the opportunity present itself, repeat what you think about yourself to someone else without, of course, revealing it as a lie. The first task in the morning and the last before bed should be to repeat these lies aloud to yourself in front of a mirror. It does not matter in the least that you know they are lies.

Commentary on the technique

This practice of "telling yourself lies" not only increases self-confidence, it also tends to reduce mental self-castigation as well. If it is practiced in combination with a general strategy of stalking, the tendency to indulge in self-deprecation can disappear altogether. This is not, as some might think, a kind of brainwashing or self-suggestion; the practitioner does not believe "the lies" are true. Rather the exercise engages the attention in a "doing" that is different from the ordinary. When the practitioner is capable of perceiving *both* as being unreal, they can be dispensed with altogether.

25. CHANGING FACADES

This is a variation of the technique "Disguises". It consists of a more or less fundamental change in appearance while still remaining functional in daily life. Although the image is changed radically, it is not meant to be carried to extremes. Following are some ways to carry out this exercise:

1. Choose a new facade. If you have sufficient energy, you can change into someone who represents all you ever wanted to be. Disguised as this new person, you can dare to do the things you always wanted to do but wouldn't permit yourself.

2. Change your physical appearance: clothes, hairstyle, way of moving about.

3. Change your personality: way of speaking, the places you frequent, your way of responding to situations.

4. Practice your new role for definite periods, lengthening them gradually as you become more proficient and begin to identify more with the new facade.

Following are some examples of the type of change implicit in this exercise: a member of a street gang who gets cleaned up, gets a haircut, begins to dress neatly, and goes back to school, studies hard, and becomes head of the class; a very preoccupied business man who disguises himself as a father who is very interested in his family, puts business matters aside, and takes his children on an excursion into the countryside; a hippie-counterculture type who dresses up to look like a young executive in a suit and tie.

INTRODUCTION FOR EXERCISES
RELATING TO DISRUPTING ROUTINES

Although "disrupting the routines of life" (III-87) is one of the basic techniques used in erasing personal history, I have singled it out here because of its importance and broad scope, as well as to stress the relative ease with which it can be applied to everyday life. It constitutes one of the fastest ways to destructure the ego and, eventually, to stop the world.

Human beings, as well as other animals, are creatures of routine. We establish them for everything: what we eat, the places we frequent, where we sleep. What we think, talk about, desire, and hate, even how we express our feelings, are converted into routines. Arriving at a place for the first time, we immediately choose a location within that, henceforth, will be "ours." If it means a certain seat, we will always try to sit in that seat.

Our routines are what make us vulnerable. Any observer is capable of detecting routines that would permit him or her to devise the appropriate traps to convert a being of routines into prey.

The routines in life are not just external activities like going to work, eating at the same hour, sleeping at the same hour in the same bed. They also include repetitive modes of behavior that we apply to everything we do. For instance, we form an idea of love (usually quite deformed) principally from our parents; during adult life, we try to reproduce that idea together with all our deformed notions about it. We may change partners, but the process repeats itself. Our tendencies toward success or failure, or cyclical crises, are expressions of our routines in life, which are manifestations of personal history. This is why we tend to have the same kinds of problems throughout our lives—lives that are nothing but repetition, treading the same path, time and time again, until we are too old and tired to continue with those old routines. Then we simply lie down and die.

The warrior, on the other hand, prefers the unlimited freedom that not having routines offers—of not knowing with precision what's going to happen; of the excitement of waking up on any given day and finding a stranger in the mirror.

Hunters can always trap their prey if they know what its routines are. But there exist magic animals that cannot be trapped, whose magic comes from the fact that their lives are free of routines. And, there are human beings who live without routines, who also are transformed into magic beings.

Routines can be detected by means of stalking exercises, such as the lists of energy expenditures and recapitulation. Once our routines are detected, we can then apply different techniques to them.

26. STALKING HABITS

Sometimes breaking routines is very difficult, since they are all that we have as ordinary people to give meaning to our lives. It is quite enough to think of routines such as boredom, anger, self-pity, smoking, overeating, or arriving late, to realize the enormous difficulty involved in attempting to break them. But it is not impossible if we have a strategy.

The principal strategy of a stalker is that you stalk yourself, your habits. You do this by quietly observing their manifestation. Thus you see how habits, or "doings," are made up of component parts. And doing, like any automatic mechanism, needs all of its parts in order to function. So if you want to stop a habit, instead of trying to force yourself to stop, merely remove one of its components and the habit cannot then be reproduced.

In order to do this, you must study all of the components of a habit that are indispensable for its production. An example is the habitual way that a man talks to his wife. Assume that he has studied this habit using techniques of stalking and has discovered that it consists of the following components:

- The subject matter of the conversation
- His wife
- His tiredness after a hard day's work
- Talking
- Saying at least once "you are wrong, dear" to his wife
- Focusing on some negative aspect of his wife
- Defending himself from any criticism on her part

This information shows many different ways he can "disarm" the habit:

- Not being present
- Sending his wife out on an errand
- Changing to a less stressful job to avoid fatigue
- Faking a toothache, an excuse not to talk
- Changing "you are wrong" to "you are right" (although it might sound absurd)
- Fixing his attention on one of her positive aspects instead of the negative
- Not defending himself; rather, telling her she is right

Another example might be smoking. The list would include cigarettes, matches, time, lack of exercise, lack of deep breaths, lack of relaxation, and stress. Then, in place of forcing ourselves to quite smoking, we simply develop the habit of climbing mountains, say, and the smoking will disappear by itself.

There is no need to eliminate all the elements of a particular "doing"; simply by removing a single element it will not be reproduced. Through stalking, any routine can be "disarmed" by the elimination of only one of its essential elements.

27. INDIVIDUALIZED NOT-DOINGS

This is one of the "most potent" techniques in the area of

stalking exercises. The name implies a specifically designed not-doing whose nature is particularly devastating to the ego of the practitioner. Its nature is to reveal what the ego really is: a description. This, of course, has a great effect on self-importance.

Here again we see the close relationship between the different techniques discussed so far and the difficulty involved in trying to fit them into a single category—especially those having to do with stalking in general and the not-doings of the personal self in particular. Recapitulation, saving energy, awareness of death, erasing personal history, losing self-importance, are all elements of this work that merge with one another to achieve a single objective: the movement of the assemblage point and acceptance of the freedom that such movement implies.

The content of the description, which is what we refer to when we say "I", is but a specific position of the assemblage point. If the assemblage point moves, the description crumbles, the ego is "stopped." In that moment we become aware of our true nature: we are luminous beings, capable of creating anything. The reality of the ego is but an illusion.

In the individualized not-doings, we are making an effort to deliberately create an illusion distinct from the personal history of the ego. With sufficient force this new illusion can replace the old one, making itself just as real within the confines of the everyday world.

This exercise can be thought of as a more advanced phase of the exercises of intending appearances, such as "Disguises" and "Changing Facades". The exercise begins with technique 22—Ego: a verbal portrait, which has already been discussed. Once you have completed your portrait, you can use it as a reference for choosing and designing an individualized not-doing for yourself. Then ask yourself impartially, referring to the person described in the portrait: What type of activity would be totally foreign to this way of being or living? What kind of activity would provoke a destructuring of this person?

Choose an activity, or series of activities, that implies working for three months to a year. Castaneda himself gave an example of this during a conversation in Mexico City. He told us that—under the direction of the sorceress Florinda—he was made to work as a cook, frying eggs for two years in an area of the United States where people of Latin descent are very much looked down upon. There he was, the famous writer Carlos Castaneda—passing for one Joe Cortez with definite Latin characteristics, receiving insults and put-downs from the clientele of the restaurant, day after day— all in order to erase his personal history and lose self-importance.

An appropriate not-doing must be radically different from what you are used to, although perhaps not quite so radical as in Carlos's case.

Following are some ways in which I have approached this technique in my workshops on stalking. Bear in mind these exercises are not well suited to beginners.

- Sent a senior executive of a corporation to beg for alms every afternoon for three months in the downtown area of Mexico City.

- Put a native Indian from the mountainous region of central Oaxaca to work as a businessman selling real estate.

- Suggested to a Mexican politician that he take some time off to work incognito as a peon in an indigenous community where Spanish is not spoken.

- Sent educated people of high social standing, who perhaps even hold positions of authority, to sell chewing gum on street corners, wash car windshields at stoplights, sell candy in the subway (which implies hiding from inspectors who are there to stop that sort of thing), perform theater works on the street, sing on city buses.

As you can imagine, save for the Indian businessman, people who are "well off" would consider such activities beyond being beneath them. These activities are normally carried out by the most impoverished in society, people who live in misery and who occupy the lowest rung on the ladder of social standing.

Once your role has been chosen, you must fulfill the following requirements:

1. Finalize to the last detail all the characteristics of the chosen role (clothes, way of speaking, tools needed, etc.). The idea is that you should appear completely natural, just one of the crowd. If you become a shoe shiner, you should strive to look like any run-of-the-mill shoe shiner, not one that stands out.

2. Practice systematically, at least four hours a day for three months.

3. Include social interaction with everyday people.

4. Strive for adequate economic returns from the activities— good income, good sales, depending on the specific activity. Remember that you possess at least the same level of efficiency as someone who does this for a living—they don't do it for fun but to subsist, and you should be capable of doing the same.

5. Avoid comforts that do not pertain to the chosen activity, such as driving to the work site, buying the merchandise from a store instead of direct from the manufacturer, and so forth.

6. Don't carry your disguise to extremes. Someone who knows you should still be able to recognize you.

7. Avoid trying to explain should you run into someone who recognizes you. Don't say, "I'm practicing a stalking exercise". Simply say, "We need more income to get ahead", or "We're out of work", or something similar.

8. Neither seek out nor avoid people who know you during the practice of not-doing.

Commentary on the technique

The results of these exercises can be ego-shattering. They demand a high grade of discipline and self-control and, as such, cannot be recommended as being suitable for beginners.

It would be ideal to practice this type of not-doing 24 hours a day for long periods, but we have found it more practical to reserve the mornings for normal daily activities and the afternoons for not-doing. This is also more convenient when other factors such as work and family are involved. Generally, a few months of not-doing will change your view of the world. Unless absolutely necessary, it is best not to inform friends or parents about what you are up to. This way you can avoid having to fight the influence of their thoughts.

Some strange things can occur using this technique, such as the case of a government worker, a participant in my workshops, whose not-doing was to sell newspapers daily in the streets of Mexico City. He was a man with many employees under him, accustomed to giving orders and having them obeyed. Nevertheless, he decided to take on the task. Each afternoon he would put on his tattered clothing and take the bus down to look for the latest edition at the newspaper's distribution center. After battling with the other vendors to become top seller, he would direct his struggle to obtain a "good corner." There he remained all afternoon, shouting at the top of his lungs amidst downtown traffic. One fine day, as he was selling his newspapers, he came face to face with one of his employees, one with whom he had much daily contact. There they were a foot apart, looking fixedly at one another. The man said that on that day he learned what fear was. He said his hair stood on end all over his body and his muscles felt as though they had been pierced by thousands of cold needles. But, as he had been working with us for some time, he knew what to do. Without taking his eyes off the man, he took a deep breath and shouted with more force than usual, *Ooovacioneeees!* (the name of a local newspaper).

The result was incredible. The employee simply did not

see him in spite of the fact that they were face to face. Something inside the employee arranged the world so as not to be able to see reality. To see his boss selling newspapers on the street was an element that did not fit in with his description of the world.

The hero of our story learned much that day about the nature of reality. He kept on working with his not-doing for several more weeks, after which he continued on his path, but the world for him was never again the same.

INTRODUCTION FOR EXERCISES RELATING TO ELIMINATING SELF-IMPORTANCE

Eliminating self-importance is the prime task of a warrior since it consumes the greater part of his or her energy. Don Juan put it this way:

> . . . in the strategic inventories of warriors, self-importance figures as the activity that consumes the greatest amount of energy, hence their effort to eradicate it. . . . One of the first concerns of a warrior is to free that energy in order to face the unknown with it . . . the action of re-channeling that energy is impeccability (VII-31).

We are not talking here about simple vanity or egocentrism—these are minor aspects of self-importance. Rather, this is a mode of perception, a specific position of the assemblage point that implies an excessive and useless waste of energy. Because of self-importance, we learn to perceive the world in such a way that we always feel the need to defend our person (ego). Because of self-importance, we remain chained to the mirror of self-reflection (the description of the ego) and we look compulsively for confirmation of this reflection in other people. Because of self-importance, we focus obsessively on the demands of ego to the point where the world is significant or meaningful only to the degree that these demands are met. Because of self-importance, we are worn out much of the time since this is the biggest energy drain. Because of self-importance we believe our problems are the most serious in existence and our opinions are the only correct ones. We are the center of the universe.

Self-importance is the throne upon which is seated everyone's personal dictator: the ego. It is through self-importance that it gains control over the entire being, to the point where we believe that we are the ego and there exist no other parts to our being. All our energy-wasting emotions and debilitating habits such as self-pity, jealousy, envy, rancor, depression, and so forth, are only possible because we feel important.

The struggle against self-importance is perhaps the most difficult of all for warriors; overcoming it signifies one of their most portentous victories.

Nearly all the exercises suggested in this book, as well as all that was taught by don Juan to his apprentice, are useful for lessening or eliminating self-importance. Special emphasis, however, should be given to the work of recapitulation, the petty tyrant, and the not-doings of the personal self as a general strategy for achieving the elimination of self-importance.

Here are a few additional techniques I have found useful. Their purpose is to diminish little by little the hegemony of self-importance.

28. TALKING TO PLANTS AND TREES

Don Juan suggested to Carlos that, in order to stop taking himself so seriously, he should begin by talking aloud to plants, an idea the apprentice found ridiculous. This simple technique is of great usefulness especially in moments when you are angry or affected by some other attack of self-importance. Choose any small plant that happens to be nearby, asking if it please would help because self-importance is such an enormous weight to carry around. This must be done aloud.

Talking to trees is similar, although, due to the empathy that trees have toward human beings, talking to them can open up even more possibilities. I have explored for many years the relation between trees and human beings and have found that they can be a tremendous help to people with particularly strong afflictions or depressions. Embrace a tree, tell it your troubles—always out loud—and it will reveal itself as a true friend who hears, understands, and responds, besides putting you at peace with yourself. As I especially love trees, I ask that anyone who practices this technique, at some later time would make an offering to a tree—water or natural fertilizer or perhaps sing to it. The tree will feel very happy.

29. ACTING FOR THE SAKE OF ACTING

Any absurd activity can serve for this technique. The important thing is to do it scrupulously, with complete attention.

As ordinary people, full of self-importance, we expect results from all our actions—some type of payment—but if we want to be warriors, then we need to learn to act for the sake of acting.

Under ordinary conditions we only act when we consider it important, always according to the dictates of the ego and its description of the world, which are also the dictates of our self-importance. Thus any action designed to reduce self-importance seems to our ego to have little importance and therefore is something to be avoided.

Acting for the sake of acting, on the other hand, offers new possibilities and experiences, allowing the unexpected to happen, teaching us to be patient, and above all to work without expectation of reward. If we cannot learn to act in a disinterested manner, then these tasks of not-doing will seem almost impossible because their results will not provide an attractive "reward" for the ego.

One way to learn to act for the sake of acting is to establish absurd routines that should be discarded once they have become habits themselves. Following are some examples:

- Say goodnight to your pillow before going to sleep.
- Walk around the block once before entering your house.
- Pile the rocks in your garden into separate groups according to size and shape.
- Take the kitchen dishes for a ride in the car once a week.

A variation would be to take on tasks that require a high degree of effort and concentration but again without thought of reward. Examples:

- Move an enormous rock for one mile and then return it to where you found it.
- Uproot a large tree stump and then replant it in the Earth.
- Carefully construct a cabin in the woods from natural materials (without destroying any living thing), make it beautiful, and when finished, tear it down without having used it, being careful to return all its components to where you found them.
- Carve a statue from wood as carefully as you can and when finished, throw it on a bonfire or in a river.

Commentary on the technique

The more time and effort spent on these exercises the more effective they will be.

30. TAKING CARE OF SOMEONE

Another useful technique for lessening self-importance is dedicating ourselves for a specific time to taking care of someone, body and soul, especially if the person is not to our liking.

For the ego—normally accustomed to taking care of its own needs—this technique can be devastating. Generally, it is best done in secret without telling the person what we are up to, unless we are dealing with a sick person or some other situation requiring the approval of the person to be cared for.

To achieve the capacity to care with true devotion and disinterest, choose a person whose care would not benefit you in the slightest degree—from your ego's point of view.

There should be no interest on your part in obtaining any-thing for yourself. Naturally, to carry this out efficiently—this strange task of caring for someone who is disagreeable, from whom you can expect no payment or compensation—you will need to learn to act outside self-importance. And this experience is well worth the effort.

31. CHANGE OF SURROUNDINGS

A temporary change of surroundings can help to dimin-ish the obsessive tendency to focus on the self. To be fruitful, however, this must be done in surroundings that are extrane-ous, unknown, and incongruent with your personal history, thus providing you with the opportunity to take yourself less seriously. For urban dwellers, spending some time in the country can be enlightening as long as you don't take all the comforts of the city, which would then not be considered a real change.

The change of surroundings to which I refer implies a true integration with the selected new surroundings, leaving behind what you were, learning a new way of being that is in agreement with the new environment.

My dealings with indigenous communities have required a radical change in my behavior and being, not in order to be accepted but simply from the standpoint of survival. One thing I discovered was that, while my old daily habits contin-ued to exert pressure on me to behave in the old way, this new world demanded completely novel ways of behaving in situations totally new to me and for which I had no routines in my old behavior to fall back on. I found myself among these people who did not speak my language, knew nothing of me or my past, in a situation that demanded that I put my self-importance to one side. While self-importance perhaps had its place in my everyday life—lending a kind of security to my existence—there in the mountains, in nature among indigenous people, it was revealed as a true extravagance and a dangerous one at that.

It is important that the chosen surroundings be as unfamiliar as possible in such a way that the people you encounter there do not in any way share the ideas you have about yourself.

32. PLAYING THE FOOL

This technique is especially for those who like to make an impression on others, for all those who have a compulsive desire to make spectators of everyone around them. These people secretly like to call attention to themselves, appearing always as the most clever, the most agile, the best athlete, the best friend, the most handsome, the most beautiful, the best lover, the one who never loses an argument. In short, those who do everything well.

One simple way of combating this compulsion is by striving to deliberately create the opposite effect. Without anyone knowing, intentionally play the part of the fool. If you are someone who is very careful and agile in your movements, begin to act clumsy, tripping over or dropping things, for example. In an argument, make ridiculous statements that make you look like an idiot, thus losing the argument. If you are identified with the well-groomed look, dress shabbily in order to appear ludicrous in places where you are accustomed to showing off.

And certainly—as Florinda stated in *The Eagle's Gift*—all those who learn to play the role of the fool without feeling hurt are capable of fooling anyone (VI-291).

33. DENOUNCING YOURSELF

This technique is a continuation of the last one but perhaps a bit more radical. While it is useful for the same type of person mentioned in exercise 32, it also can help those people whose self-importance habitually takes the form of thinking or saying terrible things about themselves, always talking to others about their tremendous sufferings, faults, or weaknesses.

Begin by finding out the most frequent thoughts or phrases you repeat to others in order to nourish your self-importance. Some common examples would be:

- Talking in such a way that others see you as a cultured or humorous person.
- Always striving to win arguments using irrefutable proof.
- Relating your impressive accomplishments.
- Making yourself interesting in order to attract a member of the opposite sex (selling the merchandise).
- Adopting the stereotype of the movie hero or heroine.
- Telling everyone your problems and tragedies in order to receive pity.

The majority of these examples involve talking, which is significant if you realize that talking is one of the basic tools you put at the service of self-importance. It is natural, since self-importance is a false report of reality, that you attempt to compose reality through talking, adjusting it to fit the peculiar form of interpretation that is self-importance.

All of these examples represent attitudes unconsciously used to project a false image, to exalt us far above what we are in reality. They consist of clichés, postures, vanity, lies, deceit—anything and everything to exalt the ego.

This exercise, then, requires you to stop them cold the moment they appear, to denounce yourself. In the middle of an argument stop yourself and say something like: "You know what? I'm stupid. I just realized I am again indulging in my old habit of arguing for the sake of arguing. You can help me by ignoring me." Or, "Stop, stop, stop. I am an imbecile; don't pay any attention to me. I ask your pardon because I realize I am just playing my old game of appearing to be intelligent in order to impress people, when in reality I am nothing more than a braggart." Or, "No, please don't listen to me anymore. I'm just indulging in my role of the suffering victim. I should shut up."

In each case, you should strive to use the most direct phrases applicable to the specific situation.

A minimum of discipline is required to practice this technique, but the results are reassuring. You begin to know ahead of time what you will say before you open your mouth. Little by little, you lose the desire to project a false image of yourself through words.

PART THREE

THE ACCESS TO THE SEPARATE REALITY

(PRACTICES FOR THE LEFT SIDE)

SIX

STOPPING THE INTERNAL DIALOGUE OR THE KEY TO THE DOOR BETWEEN THE WORLDS

THE EMPTY MIND

The possibility of silencing thoughts is most frequently encountered in the many forms of knowledge with which the West is only marginally familiar.

In conditions of everyday life, we find ourselves thinking. I do not refer here to what could be considered the systematic exercising of true reason but rather the simple act of uncontrolled thinking that we do all the time. We are always talking to ourselves in our thoughts. This what don Juan termed "the internal dialogue" (IV-20), and its suspension forms one of the central points of his teaching.

Since we are always talking to ourselves, we consider it a natural and inevitable condition of human life. We unconsciously assume that this dialogue will be shut off only after death and that the possibility of a totally "blank" mind cannot exist. This belief is further reinforced by the fact that many who do try to shut their minds off often fail in the attempt. Methods for achieving the empty mind are quite unusual and require a systematic effort.

However, seen from a more general historic and geographic angle, we have always had some interest in the possibility of achieving silence of the mind. I would say that every human being secretly yearns for this knowledge. The work of Castaneda presents the idea that, ages ago, people lived much closer to the knowledge of inner silence. We only gradually forgot what we knew due to the development and later hegemony of rational thinking (VIII-169–170), which took complete hold in the experience of the individual. In the majority of people, as time went on, thinking became more mechanical and less rational.

THE VIEW TO THE EAST

Oriental thought in general, and Hindu yoga, Japanese zen, and Chinese taoism in particular, has made the empty mind or the state of no-mind one of their basic objectives.

In Western mentality the possibility of achieving such a state, and what this would imply in the experience of the individual, has not aroused much scientific interest. We do, however, have to recognize the valiant endeavors of anti-psychiatrists whose work, lying on the borderline between formal science and marginal science, has come close to producing a state of no-mind, an experience they categorize under the general heading of "the destructured experience."[11]

When Western thought attempts to criticize itself, it looks timidly toward Oriental thought, visualizing a world divided in an Oriental/Occidental dichotomy. This leaves out of the

---

[11] See David Cooper, *La Muerte de la Familia*, Barcelona: Ariel, 1985.

scene many peoples who developed along different lines and whose view of the cosmos lies outside that of either Eastern or Western ways of thinking.

THE VIEW TOWARD THE AMERICAN INDIAN

This includes all the American Indian peoples who, from Alaska to Tierra del Fuego, created their own great civilizations in the past. Their philosophical and magical-scientific knowledge remains yet undetected by anthropologists and ethnologists of our time.

The technical superiority in conquistadors' weaponry, by which they were able to overpower the Indians, caused them to discard beforehand all possibility of learning from these Indian cultures. They could not conceive of the existence of technical or spiritual development on the part of pre-Columbian peoples, vanquished in the sixteenth century, and remaining today on the lowest rung of the evolutionary ladder—according to the logic that puts European civilizations at the top.[12]

So little is known of ways to achieve, and the results of, a state of no-mind according to Oriental mentality and practice, and even less is known about said state in the experience of the American Indian.

In reality, the state of suspended thought exists as a possibility for any human being regardless of when and where it is encountered. This knowledge recurs anywhere there is a genuine interest in self-knowledge.

DON JUAN AND THE TOLTEC HERITAGE

The Mesoamerican world contains one of the human groups that had a great interest in the state of inner silence— the historical and cultural matrix of the Toltecs. Many of their

---

[12] This vision of human development is known in the history of ethnology as "evolutionism". Although it has been severely criticized, in practice anthropologists, government officials, and missionaries continue to maintain an attitude of superiority in their dealings with native cultures, virtually the same attitude that originally gave rise to the concept of evolution.

large and almost incomprehensible works such as pyramids, sculpture, paintings, and poems, stand to the present day as testimony to their incursions into the world of inner silence and the second attention.

The teachings of don Juan Matus are clearly written in the Toltec tradition. They reveal aspects of it that remain invisible to external observers, even when they are allowed direct access to those indigenous communities of the Toltec culture surviving today—such as the Nahuas, the Huicholes, and the Maya.

In don Juan's teachings, stopping the internal dialogue is the key to the door between the worlds and one of the principal aspects of its knowledge. This is why many of the practices that his apprentice undertook were directed toward this search for inner silence, although on many occasions the sorcerer used the strategy of singling out a specific object for such practices. He didn't do this just for fun; don Juan knew that one of the worst ways to stop thoughts was to think about stopping them. And in this also lies our modern difficulty in obtaining results of this kind.

BEYOND DESIRE

In Western mentality, we are trained to think that the attainment of an objective supposes, in the first place, that we understand and know what such an objective consists of. And in the second place, that attaining such an objective is worth the trouble, creating in us the desire to achieve it. Of course, desiring it implies thinking about it—thinking that we desire it, that we want to achieve it. The uselessness of such mental activity results from making thinking the objective of desire and therefore of thought as well. This path is a mental labyrinth from which there is no escape.

Oriental teachings insist on the value of eliminating desire. Westerners might think that such an achievement would make them into apathetic and passive persons, incapable of doing or enjoying anything. Quite to the contrary, however. What Oriental teachings realize is the intrinsic relation between desire and thought: one serves as the motive force for the other.

Don Juan was also aware of this and therefore taught Carlos—among other things—to stop his internal dialogue. Carlos was tricked into believing he was doing it to fulfill some other purpose—acting for the sake of acting, or learning to do things without expectation of reward. So Carlos carried out a number of absurd tasks without any apparent objective (VI-232–233).

Acting for the sake of acting, by the way, I have labeled as *acting purposefully*. It provides the material base from which to construct the door that leads to freedom.

THINKING ABOUT NOT THINKING

It is not possible to stop thinking by thinking about it. Western rationality simply does not work as a method for achieving inner silence. To begin with we do not understand what inner silence consists of because we do not have or do not remember any experience connected with this state. It cannot be thought about because when we do, we are always thinking something different, and the experience of silence does not enter into the realm of thought. Thought cannot speak of something that is outside its sphere.

This should be made clear: thought is one of humanity's most useful tools, but its sphere of action, while very large, has definite limits. The problem is, we are so closely tied to that sphere that we finish our lives without ever knowing of the existence of other realms outside it, those which can be revealed to us precisely by stopping the internal dialogue.

So, if we cannot understand it beforehand, if by desiring it we separate ourselves from it, if by thinking about it we are really thinking about something else, then it becomes clear that we cannot stop the internal dialogue through intellectual means. Stopping thought is not something we can think about or understand; it implies action, acting for the sake of acting, acting without hope of reward. We need to achieve the experience of silence without using the straight line of reason. We need the strategy of a sorcerer without the sorcerer. The section on techniques will outline a method for setting up such a strategy for ourselves. Or to be more precise, for the ego, which is our biggest obstacle on the path to the world of inner silence.

Before that, I wish to point out some relevant aspects which we have discovered in our search and encounter with silence, that offer modern humans the possibility of recovering the forgotten world of silenced thoughts.

THINKING IS NOT PERCEIVING

The first thing to stress is that thinking is not perceiving. *Thinking is not perceiving.* As human beings we can think and we can perceive. The problem is, even though our intimate natures as fields of energy mean we are natural perceivers, we are so tied to our thoughts that we do not perceive our possibilities as such.

This is not by accident. Thought is what makes up the basic nature of the ego. In fact, thoughts are the substance of the ego. Therefore, stopping the internal dialogue allows us to leave the confines of the ego, freeing ourselves from the personal history that it sustains and that, in its turn, sustains the ego itself.

As average people, we perceive so little that we have since forgotten the distinction between thought and perception; we believe that what we think is what we perceive. Projecting our thoughts onto external reality, we substitute what we think about reality for reality itself, a continuous process that leaves us very far from perceiving the real world. In Oriental teachings, this is referred to as *maya* (illusion) or ordinary reality, the veil that must be lifted in order to see the world as it truly is. Don Juan also talks about seeing as one of the experiences that turns an average man into a man of knowledge.

We modern humans live as prisoners in a reality constructed for us by our thoughts—thoughts that are predetermined for us by the tonal of the times and by our personal history.

THE DOOR OF PERCEPTION

If we do not perceive people, things, or the situations in which we find ourselves, but instead see or believe what our thoughts dictate to us—which we continually project toward the exterior world—then it must be true that the suspension of thought represents the open door to perception.

If we perceive things as they really are, whether people, situations, events, or our own selves, we will be in a better position than someone who substitutes thoughts in place of reality. People who do not perceive find themselves struggling to control an imaginary reality and suffering the consequences of the inconsistencies between what they think is there and what is actually there.

This is what causes the crises that crop up in everyone's life from time to time. These are the moments when reality goes counter to our explanations and expectations, when, in spite of all our efforts, events don't turn out as we think they should. Then we discover that life, people, and what we feel, are not in agreement with the description that was taught us from infancy, that description we doggedly keep on trying to adjust to, without ever achieving complete success.

Our concepts about life, love, a mate, success, progress, and all of the values that we regard as being the ideal, are thus revealed as a mental fog. We give reality to these ideas and thoughts because of our insistence on behaving in agreement with the description that was taught to us. Only we discover later that it is difficult to make our lives fit into this description. In any event, it is much too impoverished and boring for all that we are able to do in our one life as mortal—and therefore magical—beings.

A person who perceives, on the other hand, can act in accordance with true reality, and thus enjoys a tremendous advantage over other human beings. This possibility, available to anyone, to lift the veil of thought and see the real world, represents power and freedom.

PASSPORT TO THE OTHER REALITY

Up to now, I have spoken of the pertinence of stopping the internal dialogue as a way of managing ordinary reality more efficiently, a fact that can be inferred from the recovery of perception implied. But the perception of ordinary reality that lies beyond the veil of thought is just the first step toward realizing the unknown possibilities of awareness. In don Juan's system of knowledge, inner silence serves as a starting point from which we can penetrate into the separate reality.

Don Juan refers to stopping the internal dialogue as the key to the door between the worlds (IV-240) because he knows that the content, limits, and form of the reality we know are products of our training from infancy. They cause us to perceive reality as we do; and the fundamental element that maintains it within these limits is the internal dialogue that, like a jealous guardian protecting his or her work, renews it with an incessant flow.

When the internal word factory shuts down, the world and our own person also cease to be and to appear exactly as we told ourselves they were. Then other facets of reality, formerly considered strange or impossible, become accessible, and this represents yet another face of true freedom. This refers to our magical heritage—to the possibility of leaving a world not of our own choosing, in which our limits are set by the tonal of the times and by personal history, and entering a world that formerly existed only in our dreams.

THE MAGIC IN THE BEYOND
AND THE MAGIC RIGHT HERE

It's true that this separate reality seems to be fantastic, if not impossible, to the average man or woman—talking to a tree, exchanging words with a whale, becoming aware of the Earth as a sentient being, acting deliberately with the *dreaming body*. It is also true that in this other reality, the confines of our way of being, acting, and feeling—determined by personal history—vanish, giving opportunities to reinvent ourselves, to discover mysterious and unknown facets of ourselves lying hidden in remote corners of our being. Once recovered, these can be integrated into a new way of living and acting in the world of everyday affairs, with new resources formerly considered out of reach.

Thus to enter into the other reality does not necessarily imply strange things such as carrying out vital objectives in the realm of dreams. They are also such unusual things as sincerely looking upon our fellows without hate, loving without slavery, discovering a new being in the mirror, daring to make a long-held dream a reality, looking at a loved one with new eyes, saying good-bye to a long-held habit we had thought to be an intrinsic part of ourselves. We will now explore some ways these might be achieved.

TECHNIQUES

One of the fundamental elements for stopping the internal dialogue is the specialized use of attention—meaning ordinary attention—which by saving energy allows the recovery of what don Juan labeled the second attention.

Since the ordinary way in which we use our attention is intimately linked to sustaining the internal dialogue, then using that attention in a nonordinary way is necessary for the suspension of the internal dialogue. In general, we will find that exercises of attention are useful for achieving inner silence and those for achieving inner silence are useful as exercises of attention, it being very difficult to distinguish between the two. Strictly speaking, the exercises for stopping the internal dialogue are really techniques for achieving the special handling of attention—a sub-area of the totality of the exercises having to do with attention. Their particular usefulness for stopping the internal dialogue explains why they are classified apart from the others.

SPECIAL USES OF THE ATTENTION

One factor that feeds the internal dialogue is that our attention is constantly focused on it. The voice of the internal dialogue is the voice of the ego, so what is occurring here is the obsessive tendency for the ego to focus on itself.

Any practice or exercise that diverts the attention from this internal word factory tends to suspend dialogue activities if the effort is sustained long enough. That is, if no attention is paid to it, the dialogue stops. Thus almost all of the exercises for stopping the internal dialogue use redirection of the attention as their key element.

Using this information as a starting point, you could make up your own exercises. Nevertheless, I will mention some of ours that have yielded fruitful results.

34. THE WALK OF ATTENTION

Walking, by itself, is good exercise that contributes to good health as we all know. But, what is not generally known is that, by adding certain special elements, we can convert a simple walk into a walk of attention. Although everyone apparently "knows how" to walk, the fact of the matter is— for modern people—to walk correctly requires special training that also tends to yield special results.

The unquestionable masters of walking are those who for centuries have walked tirelessly over the surface of the Earth, over the paths of the being they love: the Indians. From them we can learn many of the elements of walking correctly.

The walk of attention is an excellent exercise for stopping the internal dialogue. Frequent practice will unfailingly produce a state of silence. Before going into detail about its many variations I will list some of its basic elements:

- Your attention is focused not on thoughts but rather on the walk itself and the elements of attention.

- Walk in absolute silence. Should it be absolutely necessary to talk, stop walking for a moment and say what needs to be said before continuing.

- Don't try to forcibly stop your thoughts; simply let them flow, listening to them as though they were just any other natural sound.

- Keep a constant rhythm while walking; speed, however, is not important.

- Synchronize breathing with walking speed.

- Concentrate breathing to make it easier to focus attention on it.

- Maintain continuous attention on the surroundings and the feelings brought up (ignore thoughts about them).

- Pay attention to what your body feels, especially in the abdominal region.

- Focus attention on sounds.

- Don't carry anything in your hands; use a backpack for carrying.

- Prolong the exercise until you reach a state of special attention; once there, you may continue indefinitely.

Commentary on the technique

The element in italics is indispensable for the practice of this exercise, while the others may be included alternately as desired, choosing only some or all of them. Maintaining scrupulous attention on all the elements at once may require a period of practice, during which only some of the elements will be used. When that has been achieved, it can then be said that you "now know how to walk."

All the elements listed above in the "basic" walk of attention also form an integral part of all variations.

One of the most surprising results of the walk of attention, including its variations, is that altered states of consciousness are generated. More commonly known as heightened awareness, they can have different levels. The more attentive and prolonged the walk, the more profound will be the effect of heightened awareness. Also frequency of practice has a direct bearing on the results obtained. All of this allows you to achieve states of nonordinary perception and sensitivity in which the possibility of silent knowledge becomes plausible.

35. WALKING INDIAN FILE

Walking Indian file is like the preceding exercise, except it is practiced by several persons. As its name indicates, it is called this because indigenous peoples—who know well how to walk and pay attention—walk in this manner. I learned it walking with them. This is one of my favorite techniques not only because it permits the sharing of many magical moments with others, but also because it makes possible the unification of the energy and attention of the participants. This tends to increase as a final result, making it more than just the sum of its parts.

Normally this is the method used for walking when a group is involved, especially in uninhabited areas and over unfamiliar terrain. This also tends to provoke the appropriate states of alertness.

The walk has particular implications among indigenous peoples and there are basic differences between them and the way a Westerner walks.

The Western attitude tends to view any trip as consisting of two main points: departure and arrival. Thus on any trip, be it walking or in some vehicle, what lies along the way is of little importance—the main objective is to arrive, the sooner the better. Walking only serves as a means for arriving, and therefore, our prevailing attitude along the way is one of impatience, of being anxious to arrive. Or, on the contrary, we feel distress for what we left behind. The fact is that modern Westerners have a serious problem locating themselves where in reality they are: here and now.

Thus, walking Western style, used simply as a means for

getting from one place to another, is tiring and we wish for it to end as soon as possible. Naturally, this produces much fatigue, a fatigue that arises mostly from wasted energy, not from the energy required for walking. This energy waste comes from focusing attention on our thoughts instead of on something real, such as the movements of the body. Walking without attention is not only exhausting; it can even be dangerous. This partially explains why people fear to walk in unfamiliar places, or to walk at night, or simply just to walk.

Typically, when we walk, we tend to think about what we left behind (the past) or imagine what awaits us (the future), but it is difficult to locate ourselves in reality (the present).

Indigenous peoples, on the other hand, after centuries of walking know that walking is the means by which one can experience being in the here and now, besides serving as a way of getting somewhere. They know that it is possible and beneficial to walk for the sake of walking, for the pure pleasure of movement.

When Indians are going somewhere, they know that the walk, long or short, consists of one step at a time. They locate themselves in the present and don't worry about the future unless they need to plan a strategy. Once that is completed, they forget about the future until it becomes the present. Therefore while walking, Indians do not look ahead or at the summit of the mountain they are climbing but rather at what is directly below their feet.

If they wish to admire the countryside, they stop walking first and only afterward continue. When Indians walk, they are walking in the here and now, not in the before or after.

This attitude is reflected in the elements of walking Indian file, which consist of the following:

1. Select a guide, anyone who knows which path to follow or who is able to assume responsibility for sensibly guiding the group over the most appropriate path according to the conditions of the moment.

2. Walk in single file; this is fundamental. Participants remain behind the one in front of them the entire time.

3. Keep a constant distance between participants; an arm's length is usually just about right. Of fundamental importance is that this distance must be maintained regardless of variations in the terrain.

4. Direct your gaze toward the ground to the step you are taking, without looking ahead or to the side. With someone at the head of the line guiding the group, there will be no need to look up. In fact, sight is of secondary importance in this exercise; it is important to perceive the event with your entire body.

5. Establish some kind of rhythm—perhaps sounds synchronized with steps or breathing. Everyone must participate for it to have value.

6. Avoid thinking about arriving; avoid looking ahead to see "how far we have to go."

7. Two people minimum are required for this exercise.

Commentary on the technique

One of the key elements in this exercise is to maintain a feeling of unity that permits the linking of attention and energy of all those participating. There are two principal elements for achieving this unity: keeping an exact distance at all times from the person ahead and incorporating a consistent rhythm among all the participants. If someone fails to maintain the distance, is distracted, or out of rhythm, the "chain" is broken and the rest of the group will not be able to reap the benefits of the group walk.

36. FOLLOWING THE FOOTPRINTS (III-157)

This is a walk in Indian file with the addition that now participants—except the leader—are to step in the footprints of the person walking in front of them.

This means that the feet of all the participants will now move together in exact synchronization—left feet at the same time, right feet at the same time, and so on. Each foot is put down in the footprint although none is visible. This means you must "visualize" the footprint and step in it.

Commentary on the technique

The key elements in this exercise are to always step in the footprint of the person in front and to maintain synchronization in the movements of the feet in spite of sudden changes in velocity or stops due to variations in the terrain. If the walking is done with concentration, such changes will not be difficult to anticipate.

The exercise should be practiced at least an hour, and it can be extended indefinitely. If the instructions are followed faithfully, it should produce a kind of "bubble of attention" that envelops the whole group. In some way, the feeling of being an individual ego is lost, while at the same time there is developed awareness of being part of a group body. The magic of all this is that we can walk for hours and hours without fatigue. We feel full of energy, complete, and renewed.

37. THE WALK OF SHADOWS

Although this exercise is quite simple, it can provoke intense states of heightened awareness. This walk is also known as "walking with the ears".

It consists of a very slow walk of attention, trying to move about like a shadow, in absolute silence, reducing the sounds you produce while walking to almost zero. Neither steps nor breathing should be audible. You should not even be able to hear yourself but be as silent as a shadow moving about. What guides movement is the work of your ears. You concentrate so much on sounds—in order to avoid them—that hearing becomes the center of your perception. Needless to say that in this form of walking, you avoid stepping on anything that is likely to produce sound; it is preferable to lift your foot before running into a branch, to go around things instead of stepping on them, to always look to step where it will make the least noise.

38. A FORM OF WALKING ACCORDING TO DON JUAN (III-35)

1. Adopt an unaccustomed posture with your hands, such as curving the fingers toward the palm, separating the middle and ring fingers from each other, or something similar. Find a position that suits you best.

2. Maintain awareness of the entire 180 degree field of vision, taking in everything simultaneously; avoid focusing on any point in particular. Your eyes should be directed straight ahead, your gaze centered on a point just above the horizon.

There are many forms of these exercises, all of them useful for stopping the internal dialogue, but in general they are variations of the basic form, so I believe that what has been outlined here is sufficient.

I wish to reiterate that the walks of attention in general and the gait of power in particular, while classified here as exercises for stopping the internal dialogue, could just as well fall under the heading of exercises of attention.

39. THE GAIT OF POWER (III-171)

This technique can only be performed in a state of inner silence. It implies the emergence of facets of the "nagual" of the practitioner—partially if he or she is a beginner, totally if a consummate master. Here, practice and available energy are the key elements. It is a technique whose practice, involving the participation of the awareness of the other self, has given us surprising results. It is not enough to present it as a simple procedure that—on the other hand—is not so simple.

In general terms, the gait of power consists of moving at great speed, utilizing an unusual energy, without depending on the five senses in the ordinary way and without acquiring prior knowledge of the terrain, even in complete darkness. It resembles a peculiar form of running or jogging. Although it can be practiced over any kind of terrain, it is usually done where the surface is uneven, with many loose rocks, on a steep slope, or when we find ourselves at night in similar areas that would be difficult to cross under normal conditions, even walking.

It should be pointed out that this is not a normal exercise, not a sport. Not everyone can do it. It is not enough to simply know the procedure. This is something unusual that the body carries out without the intervention of the intellectual center. Putting it into practice will depend principally on the level of available energy and ability; nevertheless, I have included it in this work since it is directed toward people with many different levels of energy and work.

While the ability to do the gait of power can come simply from having practiced other less complicated techniques, there also are exercises that allow us to approach the exercise gradually, that can indicate to us if we are ready for it.

The gait of power is something that belongs to the body's unknown possibilities—in reality, all of us know how to do it, or it would be more precise to say our bodies know how. Average people, however, find themselves so disconnected from what the body knows, having lived exclusively according to the whims of the ego via the internal dialogue, that they find it almost impossible to recover this knowledge. Occasionally, people in life or death situations or some other dangerous predicament have been known to enter into the gait of power and save themselves by running in complete darkness, or over rugged terrain near drop-offs without realizing it and without the use of any procedure. When phenomena of this nature occur, they are often considered miracles or some kind of divine intervention by people looking for some way to explain the marvels that can occur when the body takes the reins.

Begin a relatively systematic practice to help the body

remember the gait of power. There are procedures for this; however these must be laid aside when the body wakes up and the gait of power begins. From this moment the body takes charge; reason and the ego with its desires and explanations are simply not invited to participate. It can be done in the following manner:

1. Begin by trotting on flat ground in daylight. Raising your knees as high as possible, continue with this until you feel that the body can carry on this way without forcing. You are looking for an intermediate point between tension and relaxation. Your muscles should warm up little by little, reaching a state of flexibility that is "tense," so to speak, and not apt to become flaccid. Should you encounter an obstacle such as a small rock, for instance, your muscles won't be so hard as to suffer contusions of a joint, or so soft that a bone becomes dislocated. You enter into a peculiar state of being that could be labeled relaxed tension in which you are awake, alert, and active but with an internal feeling of sobriety and control. This step should be practiced for periods of at least an hour.

2. As you begin to feel comfortable with the first step, then start practicing under more rigorous conditions such as level but more irregular terrain, rocky terrain with average size rocks, or a dry river bed. Also gradually increase your velocity. The important thing is to feel natural since forcing yourself when feeling insecure can cause injury. Notice how flexibility in the legs allows them to adjust naturally over rocks, fallen tree trunks, or other obstacles. Little by little, try to sense the terrain with your body while avoiding excessive use of your eyes to guide your feet. Your gaze should be relaxed and directed toward the area of ground in front of you but without focusing on specific points. Consider that in normal walking the decisions of where and how to place the feet are made according to the relationship of sight/brain/mind. The gait of power, on the other hand, functions from the relationship of body/world, or, to be more precise, as "energy from the inside/energy from the outside".

When you have achieved great speed over the type of terrain just described, sweeping the ground with your gaze, maintaining rhythm and equilibrium without becoming exhausted, falling, or hurting yourself, you will be ready for the next phase.

3. In this step you can begin to practice on sloped terrain—at first gentle slopes, then steeper ones. As your ability increases, look for steep slopes with irregular terrain. If you begin by practicing on paths, you will have more control across open country. Remember, this is a process not normally learned in one day; rather it requires constant practice. The time it takes depends on each person. And, there exist no limits to what can be achieved with the gait of power, nor to the transformations that can be experienced. When working on this type of terrain, it is very important not to overdo it. Nothing can be achieved through great velocity if you lose rhythm and security— then you would fall into the confines of the ordinary and could be injured.

4. Using all the techniques described so far, begin to deliberately change velocity, according to the variations of the terrain, while maintaining the same rhythm. At this point, be sure to include more or less steep slopes in your practice.

The following instructions are only for those who have attained a high degree of facility in the preceding four steps and are ready to practice in the dark of night.

5. Begin by practicing at sunset or under a full moon over known terrain. The full moon is especially desirable because of the light it affords, and because its presence facilitates entry into left-side awareness. As you gain proficiency, then attempt to do it on a totally dark night over unfamiliar terrain. However, when you reach this level, you no longer find yourself—as an ego—voluntarily carrying out an exercise. Rather it is your body that acts according to a direct relation it has with the world, beyond the boundaries of reason.

Commentary on the technique

Since the internal dialogue and the gait of power are events that cannot take place simultaneously, we should have begun to notice, almost from the start, that the dialogue tends to stop without any direct intervention on our part. As the gait of power demands the participation of all our energy, there is none left over to keep the internal dialogue going. This is what makes the technique infallible. If we keep on thinking, however, it means we are merely engaged in jogging, not in the gait of power.

In my workshops, participants are encouraged to listen attentively to the messages of their bodies which consist of feelings rather than thoughts or ideas. These messages are in reality part of the silent knowledge that is our birthright as human beings, to which, unfortunately, we rarely listen. For those exercises involving the gait of power, it must be stressed that no participants should force themselves to practice techniques that are yet beyond their ability to perform. An example of this would be a group using the gait to descend a mountain. If one or two members clearly felt they were unable to keep up with the rest, then by no means should they try. Clear signs of this type of situation would be loss of breath, tendency to stumble, loss of equilibrium. In such cases it is better to slow down until equilibrium and rhythm are restored.

As has been stated, the practice of the gait of power implies stopping the internal dialogue. This puts us in contact with unknown facets of the world and our own being. Achieving inner silence during intense physical activity, while interacting with the world of nature, opens the door to the irruption of states having to do with the awareness of the other self. Nagualism is one of its possibilities.

AN ILLUSTRATION OF THE RELATIONSHIP
BETWEEN THE GAIT OF POWER AND
THE PHENOMENON KNOWN AS NAGUALISM

Doing the gait of power, especially in uninhabited areas at night, it is not uncommon to feel as though we become transformed into some type of animal. It can be felt by the change in breathing, in the security with which we move, and in the sounds we involuntarily emit.

I discovered this once working with a group as we walked Indian file over an enormous hill south of Mexico City. It was at night under a full moon. We had been working for two days in a series of exercises outside the confines of the verbal—an activity we call "tribes." On this nocturnal walk there was a feeling of peace, of being enveloped by the darkness, and we were a group of shadows moving about in our natural habitat. Our strange costumes, two days without speaking one word of a known language, and the intense level of work to which we had submitted, had brought us to a peculiar state of being in which ego and personal history were not functional. We were a tribe, and we had to reach the territory of another tribe that lived on the opposite side of the mountain.

Suddenly, I felt a certain urgency that made me increase my pace. The surrounding vegetation seemed to blur together and the world became darker. It was as though something were pulling me; as if it wanted to pursue, to reach something unknown. Little by little, I began to jog and a rhythm took hold of me. I felt I could trot or run as long as was necessary. I knew I wouldn't trip even though I could only perceive shadows around me. I tried to get the group to follow me. I tried "pulling" them to no avail until what was pulling me overcame my efforts and I experienced a type of vertigo. I began jogging faster, it turned into a run, then I took off running in complete darkness across an open field, at a velocity I would not have achieved on flat level ground in broad daylight. My breathing became deep and savage. My body emitted strange grunts and pantings. I was converted into an animal running through the mountains—an animal in its element. The shadows had meaning for me. It was natural to move about in this medium. It was my medium. I was born for this, although I had not known it until now. Everything was a mystery and a discovery. Everything was magic and power. I experienced the joy of another world, being a savage animal without thoughts, without history. I knew which animal it was and I knew that I would always secretly be that animal during my life on Earth.

A lot of time passed before I became myself again and found my companions. I never wondered how I would have appeared to spectators. I suppose it would have depended on their sensitivity and capacity to "see". An average person would have been frightened. As for myself, I have no doubt what occurred. Don Juan was right: there exists no reality beyond what we feel. Reality is a feeling. That night, running as a wild animal through the mountains, I discovered the principle of nagualism.

SPECIAL USE OF THE SENSES

Since the internal dialogue functions hand in hand with the ordinary way in which we use our five senses, then a modification in the way we use our senses can help us to achieve silence.

In the consumerism of modern society, the sense of sight could well be called "the king of the senses." The whole system of consumerism depends on visual impact as the key element. Therefore, for ordinary people, the other senses take second place. So under the spell of sight are we that we hardly pay attention to what our other senses could reveal to us. And this occurs because the sense of sight has become the docile servant of the internal dialogue.

The everyday relation between the senses and the internal dialogue could be expressed thus: eyes, thought, world, eyes, and so on. What we see, and the way in which we see it, is maintained by the internal dialogue in such a way that reality is not meaningful to us from the outside. We project it from the inside onto our exterior reality in order to later perceive this reflection of ourselves, without ever realizing it. Since we have trained the sense of sight to aid us in this process, if we force it to perceive in a different way, or if we change the normal hierarchy in the use of our senses, we can stop our internal dialogue. An example of this, already mentioned, would be the walk of shadows in which hearing and touch capture the attention that normally we give only to sight. Any unusual use of the senses can serve as an exercise for achieving inner silence.

40. LISTENING

Remain in complete silence with your eyes closed for periods of at least 15 minutes, listening to the sounds entering your ears (II–225).

41. THE FLOW OF NATURE

In the same manner as the previous exercise, this time use an uninterrupted but variable sound such as a river flowing, the crackling of a campfire, the sound of the wind or the rain.

42. LISTENING TO SILENCES

Listen to the sounds in natural surroundings, trying to detect the spaces of silence between them until you can distinguish a rhythm of sounds as well as a rhythm of silences. Try to link perceptually the moments of silences, much as you normally do with sounds (II-225–232).

43. TEMPORARY BLINDNESS

Remain blindfolded for periods of several hours to several days, while trying to remain active. This technique requires the presence of another person to avoid risky situations.

44. UNFOCUSED VISION

Look with your eyes out of focus, taking in all the elements in your field of vision without focusing on any one element in particular. Practice for periods of 15 minutes minimum (V-295–296).

45. OBSERVING SHADOWS

Look at objects containing areas of shadow, such as trees, large rocks, or mountains, trying to visually group together the areas of shadow so as to perceive the object as an ensemble of shadows instead of a mass of light and color (III-194).

Commentary on the techniques

As in the majority of these techniques, constant practice plays an important role. The more practice the better the results. The only limit might be if, before cessation of the internal dialogue is achieved, we should find ourselves falling into some kind of maladjustment with the world of everyday affairs. In such a case the length and frequency of our practice should be reduced. Any anxiety should be avoided during these exercises. This can best be achieved by performing them as though they were an end in themselves, forgetting that they are a means for something more. Forget that their real purpose is to stop the internal dialogue. Another important factor is finding the time and space in which to do this type of work. The appropriate time would be that in which we are not concerned with anything else—a length of time specifically set aside for practice. We can do them anywhere, but it is best to begin in areas removed from places we frequent in everyday life—perhaps uninhabited areas out in the country. In later stages, when we are more advanced, it is advantageous to work in the city.

BREATHING

The majority of special breathing techniques are useful in silencing the mind, since they direct our attention to breathing rather than thoughts. Focusing attention on breathing is in fact one of the basic general forms for achieving silence. This is why many meditation techniques can be appropriate, especially if we avoid associating them with religion, esotericism, symbolism, or other isms.

46. BASIC BREATHING TECHNIQUE

Also known as the complete breath, this exercise consists of the following elements:

1. Inhale and exhale through your nose.
2. Upon inhaling, fill your abdominal region first, then your chest, starting from the bottom and working up.
3. Fill your lungs completely, until there is absolutely no more room for air.
4. Hold the air for a moment before exhaling to insure complete oxygenation.
5. When exhaling, make sure to expel all the air, leaving your lungs completely empty.
6. Inhale and exhale slowly. A breathing rate somewhat slower than normal should be sufficient.
7. Focus on breathing, not on thoughts. Should thoughts occur, simply hear them as though they were a sound without any significance whatsoever. Attention should be maintained on breathing.

47. VARIATION OF THE BASIC BREATHING TECHNIQUE

Use the same technique as before, except exhale through your mouth. The state of attention produced is distinct, best suited for situations requiring great intensity.

48. VARIATION WITH SOUND

Use all the basics of the complete breath, but direct all of your attention to exterior sounds. With the totality of your being, inundate your interior world to such an extent that there is no room left for thought. For this you can use the sounds of nature or the sounds of the city. Music can also be used, especially if there are no words to start you thinking. A more complicated but useful variation of this would be to tune in on a discussion, paying attention only to the sounds of the words but avoiding their meaning at all costs. That is, listen to the words as if they were just sounds (difficult for beginners).

49. VARIATION USING NUMBERS

This is like the basic technique, but now assign the number one to inhaling, and the number two to exhaling. Together with all the other elements of the complete breath, do this variation in the following manner:

1. During inhalation, visualize and pronounce mentally the number one.

2. During exhalation, visualize and pronounce mentally the number two.

When steps one and two can be performed without interference from thoughts, go on to steps three and four.

3. Simply visualize the number; don't pronounce it to yourself mentally.

4. Now eliminate visualization of the numbers as well, leaving all the attention for "contemplating" the inhalation and exhalation. If the mind starts thinking, go back to the previous steps.

50. THE CANDLE OF SILENCE

This technique deals with doing the complete breath in a darkened room, contemplating the flame of a candle made and molded by you while you were in a state of total concentration. Attention must be on the flame and breathing If you feel you are on the verge of thinking, fill your mind with an image of the flame, thus leaving no room for thoughts. Depending to what degree your thoughts have been calmed, return attention to the exterior flame. Alternate between the external and imaged internal flame as needed, thus intercepting thoughts before they take concrete form. The more attention and care you invest in the fabrication of your candle, the more effective it will be in "pulling" your attention. With this in mind, you can even make a work of art out of the candle; the more intricate its elaboration, the more useful it will be.

Commentary on the techniques

These techniques can be done with eyes open or closed, although at the beginning they are best done with the eyes closed for better concentration. Except for the practice of listening to sounds, a quiet place is recommended, or one with relaxing sounds. Practice periods should last for a minimum of 15 minutes.

It should be mentioned that smoking—besides being harmful to health—severely affects breathing, perception, inner silence, and awareness. The explanation is very simple. Anyone who has practiced any kind of controlled breathing knows the close relation between breath and perception, between breath and awareness. Those who smoke cannot breathe well; therefore their possibilities of awareness and perception will be limited to a great degree in comparison to those who do not smoke. For those wishing to stop the internal dialogue, the breathing exercises will lose much of their effectiveness if the lungs are filled with nicotine. He or she who sincerely wishes to be able to see in the donjuanist meaning of the word would do well to begin by giving up smoking.

51. ARTS AND SPORTS

Depending on the degree to which its practice is connected with feelings rather than thoughts, any sincere artistic activity can bring us near to silence—especially any that do not require the use of language. Particularly useful are the art of dance and the playing of a musical instrument, since their practice involves a high degree of concentration. In reality, all forms of real art come from the world of inner silence—even true theater, as was mentioned in the chapter on stalking.

This refers, of course, to art done for the challenge and the mystery it implies, not art done solely for exhibition or to awaken admiration in others. It is unfortunate that our modern consumer-oriented society is accustomed to labeling as art a great number of vulgar manifestations of megalomania. Many individuals, through mental illness or simple economic interest, are compelled to believe they are artists, pretending to sing, paint, or act, when in reality what they are looking for is to sell themselves at the best price on the garbage market. All of this produces an art that, in the final analysis, is not art at all.

Much the same phenomenon occurs in the world of sports. We should discard from the beginning all of that which, in the name of sport, involves exhibitionism and unlimited desire for profit—such as televised sport.

Natural sport, on the other hand, done for pleasure and challenge is highly beneficial for our body (but not for the ego), not only for health reasons. Since it requires reactions and reflexes faster than we can think, it gives an opportunity to act for reasonably long periods without the intervention of the internal dialogue. It has the additional advantage of putting us in contact with our corporeal being, letting us rest temporarily from the tyranny of the ego. Especially beneficial are those sports that involve integral and respectful contact with nature, taking care of course not to damage her—which is also a way of avoiding damage to ourselves.

SEVEN

THE MAGIC OF ATTENTION

PERCEPTION AND ATTENTION

Attention is one of the key words found throughout the works of Carlos Castaneda.

The specific way in which we use our attention causes us to perceive reality in the way we do. In that sense, attention sustains the world.

Attention is that property of awareness that causes us to focus on certain aspects of internal or external reality while discarding others. But in the donjuanist vision of reality, as in modern physics, there is much more to the world than what is perceived normally; in fact, it contains an infinite number of elements that escape our perception.

For modern physicists and chemists, technology has served as a way of perceiving and manipulating certain aspects of this "invisible reality"—such as radio waves, radiation, or television signals. The sorcerer, on the other hand, since time immemorial has used another tool for witnessing and manipulating this separate reality: the magic of attention. Human perception has been trained to function in a selective way not determined by biological factors; the result is the everyday way in which we see the world. The way we use our attention is precisely the result of that training, through which all new human beings must pass as they enter into contact with other human beings who already perceive reality in a certain way due to this very same training. The process of attention, which is properly said to be a flow, implies an intricate process of selection—what Castaneda terms "skimming" (VI-284, in Spanish language editions only). Skimming refers to the process of choosing to perceive certain elements of reality while discarding others, in a universe of practically infinite perceptual possibilities, in such a way that what results is an orderly perception of reality, not chaos.

The magic of attention consists of giving order and meaning to everything we perceive. Apart from selecting what we perceive, it also refines the details of any given object in such a way as to agree with the perception of other human beings. However, adult human beings may agree on how they perceive a given object but the same object would be perceived differently by animals who do not pass through the process of human socialization. Infants, on the other hand, are born with raw animal perception. They haven't yet learned the magic of attention that will arrange their perception in terms that will permit them to function in the world of everyday affairs with the other members of their species.

ATTENTION AND ITS LIMITS

A small child functions with a perception much less restricted than that of an adult. Therefore, oftentimes the child will perceive aspects of reality that adults can no longer see, that they would discard as childish fantasies. Nonorthodox modern psychology has given credit to observed phenomena in the peculiar world of infantile perception. An example can be found in the dermal/optical phenomenon (visual perception through the skin) in which any child with the proper training is capable of seeing and reading with the hands or feet. Not long ago I witnessed a child play a game of dominos blindfolded. He did not require the use of his eyes to see. However, the schools that teach this do not admit adults. They say that in general only children are capable of learning this technique.[13] Adults, due to the unconscious training of their attention, are already firmly fixed to the limits and specific modes of perception, while children enjoy much greater freedom in this regard.

In the world of don Juan, the sorcerers and apprentices are warriors struggling to rescue this possibility of using their perception in new ways, much like what we knew as infants, to aid them in penetrating into other worlds.

Once we learn, due to the force of our attention, to perceive in the way we do, we also cancel out—almost always permanently—the possibility of ever perceiving anything beyond what our attention permits us. We can, however, involve ourselves in a consistent and disciplined work in order to break our perceptual barriers.

Don Juan's proposition is that deep inside all of us lies the latent ability of our awareness to focus itself on unusual aspects of the world—on the unknown—that we normally do not even suspect exist.

THE FIRST AND SECOND ATTENTION

The way in which we use our attention in everyday life is known in the work of Castaneda as the first attention (V-266). This is what we use to perceive and impart order to our everyday world. The majority of people only know and have developed this form of attention, which keeps closed that door that opens the way to the separate reality. Castaneda also indicates the existence of another form, called the second

---

[13] In Mexico, this phenomenon is widely known, since these dermal/optical schools periodically advertise on television to promote their courses.

attention (V-266), which represents an unknown and very specialized use of the attention. It permits us to perceive another, practically limitless, part of reality that could well be called another world since it is so foreign to our world of everyday affairs.

The two attentions operate in coexisting parallel areas of reality that normally never come into contact. That is why Castaneda states that the first and second attention are separated by "parallel lines" (VI-292, in Spanish language editions only). To illustrate the perceptual difference between the two attentions I will take the perception of the human body: in the first attention it is seen as the physical body we all know; in the second it is seen as the famous cocoon or luminous egg so often mentioned by don Juan.

THE FIXATION OF THE ATTENTION

Another characteristic of either first or second attention is its ability to summon events. People in general do not perceive this, and attribute much of what happens to them as good luck or adversity. Without ever suspecting, they obsessively focus their attention on things, objects, situations, or people through fear, attachment, desire, or curiosity, and unconsciously summon these events to their lives. Also, excessive fixation of the second attention can provoke unusual effects, similar to what has taken place among sorcerers and seers—especially the old seers—creating an endless supply of magical objects for all kinds of purposes, from small amulets to great pyramids (VI-17).

The recovery of the second attention and its integration with the first implies, according to Castaneda's work, entry into the mysterious and practically unthinkable third attention also known as total freedom (VI-294, in Spanish language editions only).

However, on a more practical level for readers of this book, a healthy approximation of the second attention could very well begin with a specialized nonordinary handling of the first attention.

NOT-DOING AND ATTENTION

Performing activities that obligate the first attention to focus itself in unusual ways on the known world, or to focus on aspects that generally go unnoticed, produces the effect of an increase and/or saturation of the attention. This can lead to states of heightened awareness and eventually to the second attention.

Of course, as were described before, the exercises of the not-doings of the personal self and stopping the internal dialogue are also exercises of attention, but their emphasis or sphere of action differs from what is described here.

TECHNIQUES

Following are some exercises that could properly be classified as exercises of attention, as well as some in which the work of Castaneda is classified simply as not-doings. These are included together here since both groups tend to produce substantial variations in perception through intentionally modifying the use of attention.

52. OBSERVING SHADOWS (III-194)

1. Find a large leafy bush.

2. Find a comfortable relaxed position in which you can concentrate.

3. Calmly observe a branch of the bush, but instead of focusing on the leaves concentrate your attention exclusively on their shadows until you find yourself looking at a "branch of shadows" in place of leaves.

4. Widen your field of view, concentrating only on the shadows.

5. Try to perceive the entire bush as a "bush of shadows".

Later stages of this exercise can be practiced using a tree and following the same procedure. Practice for 30 minutes minimum.

53. OBSERVING ROCKS (III-203–206)

Another way of working with shadows is with rocks.

1. Observe a small pebble placed on top of a larger rock. A large flat rock where you can lie face down would be ideal. Your face should be about 8 inches from the pebble. Concentrate on the pebble, looking at it in detail, trying to discover its cavities and holes, observing all the small details inside. Concentrate until all of your attention is absorbed by the pebble. Observe it until it fills your entire field of vision.

2. Next, focus your attention on the shadow cast by the pebble, perceiving it as a fluid that keeps the pebble and the rock glued together, until they appear as one.

3. Following what Castaneda presents in *Journey to Ixtlan*, (III-210) continue your observation of shadows, using large rocks. You need two large rocks or boulders that cast long and more or less parallel adjacent shadows. Find a comfortable relaxed position looking at the two shadows simultaneously, trying to unite them perceptually by crossing your eyes but keeping the images in focus until the shadows are superimposed on one another.

Try this by placing two expertly chosen small or medium size rocks in an appropriate spot in which to do the exercise. For some people this seems to work better than with very large rocks.

54. THE TREE MADE OF SKY

This variation of the preceding exercise has given us very good results.

1. Find a leafy tree of medium height, preferably one you

like at first sight. If the tree forms part of a larger group that casts a large shadow, so much the better. You must be able to see patches of sky between the leaves but not direct sunlight, so as not to injure your eyes.

2. Sit or lie down underneath the chosen tree. Of course you must be comfortable. Look at the branch structure of the tree, but in place of seeing branches and leaves, focus your attention on the spaces between them. Try to perceive this group of spaces as a whole, like you normally do with the branches and leaves. If the background sky is blue, you will, little by little, begin to perceive "a tree with blue leaves", or pieces of blue scattered over a green watery background. You must be relaxed and able to concentrate while avoiding the tendency to zero in on specific details, striving instead to take in everything entering your field of vision. Once perception is altered and you find yourself viewing something like the tree with blue leaves, practice paying attention to details in the scene. Avoid focusing on them directly, since this would break the spell of your not-doing.

55. WALKING BACKWARD (VI-124)

This simple technique can be practiced over almost any kind of terrain, depending on the ability of the participant.

The exercise entails walking backward without turning around to see where you are going. In the beginning, practice on flat level ground without dangerous irregularities, only gradually increasing the degree of difficulty as you continue the practice.

1. Walk backward, having someone there to guide you. The exercise is done in complete silence to aid in concentration and sensitization. The person guiding walks facing you as you walk backward; if there should be an irregularity or an obstacle, the guide will indicate with hand signals whether to go to the right, to the left, or stop. Do not look

behind you, only at the hands of the person guiding. Practice for at least 20 minutes, after which the roles of guide and walker can be reversed.

2. This is done like the first step, but without a guide. Your guides are, initially, your knowledge of the terrain and its characteristics, which you will no doubt have noticed in looking down at the terrain in front of your feet. Now, little by little, try to sense the terrain behind you with your entire body. Practice for 15 minutes minimum.

3. This is done in the manner of step one, but now begin to trot backward, slowly at first and then as you gain confidence, increase speed until you are going at an all-out run.

4. This is done like step three, but without a guide.

5. Take extended walks backward in the country, down a known path. After one or two hours of this, you should be soaked in not-doing.

6. Walk backward, but in a group. This can add an enormous quantity of extra attention to each participant, but it requires that all work with the same level of intention and concentration.

Commentary on the technique

One principal aspect of this technique is that it can teach us to perceive the exterior world without depending so much on our eyes. Therefore, it is very important to resist the impulse to turn around. Each time we turn around, we interrupt the process of sensitization that the body goes through in order to adjust to the experience. Turning around converts the situation into something ordinary, and we have to start again from the beginning. However, becoming sensitive does not mean "perceiving with the back". We are not trying to visualize what lies behind us, as that would keep us dependent on our eyes. Rather we are looking for a feeling of security emanating from corporeal consciousness using nonvisual stimuli. The reality is that the entire body is capable of functioning as a perceiver—not just the eyes alone. The correct attitude is one of patience, relaxation, and—if possible—inner silence.

56. THE HAT WITH MIRRORS (VI-137)

Find a suitable hat and attach two mirrors to it. Any hat with a brim or sun visor will do. From the brim hang two small mirrors 4 to 6 inches from your face and a little to one side of your direct line of sight in such a way that you can see behind yourself. It is important that the mirrors not obstruct your vision ahead; they should be positioned so as to provide you with the widest field of vision both in front and behind. The mirrors can be mounted by means of wires, or screws, or any system that will hold them firmly against any possible movement.

With the hat finished, you can now practice the following exercises:

1. The basic exercise consists of walking backward using the mirrors for guidance. The more you practice, the more attention and skill you gain, allowing you to walk over irregular terrain, out in the country, or on gentle slopes. The degree of attention you are looking for is achieved when you can look simultaneously in both mirrors and integrate the separate images so that they form a single field of vision, exactly as you do when your eyes are looking forward.

2. This is the same as the preceding step, but now you include the field of view in front of you as well, keeping in sight the field of view behind you, and all the while walking backward.

3. Nocturnal practice: Follow the instructions as in step one, but do it at night. The ideal place for this would be a forested area or a desert. Begin slowly, giving yourself time to get used to walking among shadows. Don't be

frightened or nervous if "strange things" are seen in the mirrors; actually it is not strange if you begin to see or experience unusual things when you behave in unusual ways.

4. Group practice: As in the majority of the walking exercises, doing it in a group can broaden the scope of the experience, as long as the group is tightly knit (everyone working equally).

A variation, only to be practiced by those with a good deal of experience, is to combine the exercises of the skeleton (explained in the section on the awareness of death) with the nocturnal exercises of the hat with mirrors. Practicing this alone is not recommended.

THE PURIFYING HARNESS

In *The Eagle's Gift*, Castaneda mentions using a harness to suspend the self above the ground as a not-doing that has the virtue of purifying the body and even curing illnesses "that are not physical . . ." (VI-184). He also says that its beneficial effect can be used to prepare the self for a difficult journey or any other experience requiring maximum effort, and he presents it in two variations: suspending from the ceiling, or suspending from the branch of a tree. Personally, I have worked more with trees, which, due to the natural affinity they have for human beings, are an immense help.

For both variations the first step is to gather the necessary materials as follows:

• A harness in which you can remain suspended for long periods without pain or discomfort. Those used in parachuting, speleology, or something similar, would work. A harness of the type used in mountain climbing is generally not as comfortable, since such an activity rarely requires remaining suspended for long periods of time. (A suitable harness can be purchased ready made at sporting goods stores or—since it is not difficult—you can make one. Borrow one to use as a model from a mountain climber, parachutist, rescue worker, or speleologist, or gather the needed information from books on the subject. The material I have used is the same as that used in auto mobile seat belts, sewn with nylon fishing line. Each seam should be sewn across at least 3 times, using a small-point stitch for maximum security.)

- High quality rope or steel cable with a resistance of at least 1100 pounds. I personally prefer rope—besides being more natural, it is lighter and easier to manage. The rope used by mountain climbers or speleologists is at least 9mm.

- Some kind of support over which to pass the rope and elevate yourself. It must be high enough, strong, and not apt to damage the rope during use.

57. SUSPENDED FROM THE CEILING

For this technique we need an appropriate place such as a warehouse, a garage, or any space with exposed overhead beams of metal or wood. The only requirements are that there be room above the beam to pass the rope and that the beam be strong enough to hold a person suspended in a harness. Instead of allowing the rope to contact the beam directly, it is much easier to tie one or two carabiners to the beam which function as supports for the elevating rope. Carabiners are a type of oval ring made of steel or aluminum with a movable safety catch that can be opened or closed. They are extremely strong and will not damage a rope—they permit it to slide without friction or fraying. They can be purchased at any sporting goods shop.

With all the necessary materials, the technique is very simple. First, pass one end of the rope over the beam or through the carabiners. Get in the harness and tie it to one end of the rope. With the combined effort of two strong persons pulling on the other end, you are elevated almost to the level of the beam. The free end of the rope is tied to some kind of anchor near the floor. You can remain suspended in this way for as long as necessary. Periods from 8 to 12 hours are usually adequate. This exercise is best done at night as that is when the ego and the ordinary way in which you see the world lose their force. When the exercise ends, you are lowered. This procedure can be repeated as often as required.

58. SUSPENDED FROM A TREE

The same materials can be used as in the previous technique with the exception of the steel cable, as trees are not overly fond of steel. Steel or no, be careful not to damage the tree in any event. The following steps will help in that regard:

1. Find a large tree with strong thick limbs.

2. Ask the tree's permission—speaking aloud—to work in it and ask its help, explaining your motives for doing so. Although it might never occur to us, it could happen that the tree would be opposed to sending any kind of sensitive message. If this is the case, you will have to look for another tree.

3. Climb up to the selected branch and prepare it for the passing of the main rope, or for that which will be used to tie down the carabiners. The preparation consists of wrapping the branch with canvas or some other type of resistant cloth, tying it securely. This is to protect the branch from injury from the main rope.

4. Once the supports are in place, pass the free end of the rope over the limb, enter the harness, and be pulled up.

5. Be very attentive to any manifestation on the part of the tree, which will react to your presence. Remember that you are inside its luminous cocoon.

6. Communicate with the tree; express your feelings or sing to it.

7. This exercise is best done in an isolated area, away from people not involved in your work.

Commentary on the technique

The technique of remaining suspended has many uses. I have used it myself and I have applied it in my work groups to treat cases of depression, disorientation, or emotional crisis. It also has served me as a preparation for camp exercises, excursions, or trips that demand more effort than normal, such as long hikes in the mountains or open desert country. The result of suspension has always been a feeling of purification and of being reenergized, of feeling much lighter.

Three elements to keep in mind while doing this exercise are: absolute silence; darkness; and maintaining a high level of concentration during the preparatory stages. The longer and higher a person remains suspended, the greater will be the effect. It is possible to find trees with suitable branches at heights of 30 feet or more. It may be practiced for several days in a row, or the participant can remain suspended day and night. In this case begin at dawn and end at dawn of the following day.

It is important not to fall asleep.[14] As a precaution, someone below can call up to the participant from time to time.

The state of awareness and perception after the hours of practicing this not-doing is quite special and should not be recklessly dissipated. Once you have descended from the harness you should strive to maintain a state of attention and silence, avoiding noisy attitudes or activities that will rapidly disconnect you from the experience.

Commentary on the exercises of attention and not-doing

These exercises should be carried out with tranquillity and without haste, since their effect is cumulative. Average people, accustomed only to "doing", can easily become bored

---

[14] It can be beneficial to sleep while suspended from a tree, even in using a hammock, but then you would be dealing with another exercise.

or fatigued with exercises of not-doing, especially if there are no quick or spectacular results. Persistence and effort are the basic factors. The effect of being immersed for hours in not-doing is manifest even in those cases where it is felt that "nothing happened".

Concentration is important and it is something that the apprentice must learn. We are accustomed to letting our attention and our thoughts wander and digress without any control on our part. Little by little, we can learn to direct our first attention and to concentrate. Only then will we come finally to inner silence and forms of attention that we did not realize existed.

EIGHT

SETTING UP
DREAMING

COMMON DREAMS

Western mentality tends to think of dreams as an illusory reality—or as not reality at all. This is just one more consequence of the modern tendency to conclude that anything that does not fit the ordinary description of reality does not exist. Therefore, dream experiences such as flying, conversion into strange beings, or talking to animals, must necessarily be discounted as being unreal.

The most that science has been able to do in giving meaning to dreams has been in the realm of psychoanalytic theory with roots in the work of Sigmund Freud in the late nineteenth and early twentieth centuries. One of the principal aspects of this theory refers precisely to the interpretation of dreams.

Leaving aside all corollaries of the second, third, and fourth levels—with their Oedipus complex, phallic obsessions, and the rest—in its most basic form the theory states that dreams are more or less symbolic expressions of a person's repressed desires, fears, and anxieties. This symbolism, which has its roots in objects of fear or desire, is not often expressed directly in dreams, but rather through images that at first glance may appear to have nothing to do with the mentioned objects. Thus, an oppressive, authoritarian father figure could appear in a dream as an enormous tree trunk that falls over on the dreamer; or a woman, desired by a man, could appear to him as a wild horse that eludes all attempts at capture.

Although most people remain ignorant of Freudian theory and its possibilities for interpreting the meaning of dreams, its basic proposition is applicable (in general terms) to the majority of people in modern society. Our dreams do indeed reflect our fears and desires.

NONCIVILIZED DREAMS

However, Freud is not the only possibility. An examination of other cultures both past and present reveals that the conclusions of this theory, like psychoanalytical theory in general, are not universal. They are not applicable to all societies in all eras. For example, take the theme of sexual repression, which held a special interest for Freud. While in European and European-based cultures, sexual repression and the consequent obsession with sex have been and still are unchanging, in some other ethnic groups with their distinct cultural orientations, there are indications of a much more open and healthy attitude toward sexuality. Many examples abound, from the Bushmen of the Kalahari Desert[15], to the Polynesians of Samoa.[16]

Also, it is easily demonstrated that not all human beings have the same type of dreams, that not all dreams are "Freudian." My personal experience among the Huichole

---

[15] G. Silberauer, *Cazadores del desierto: cazadores y habitat en el Desierto de Kalahari*, Barcelona: Mitre, 1983.

[16] Margaret Mead, *Adolescencia, Sexo y Cultura en Samoa*. Buenos Aires: Paidos, 1979.

Indians, for example, has permitted me to observe the special interest they have in their dreams. It is very common to find a father asking his small son who has barely learned to talk: "What did you dream, my son? Remember, remember well, what did you dream?" In this way, the Huicholes begin very early to pay attention to their dreams, an ability that not only facilitates remembering them but also gives their dreams a pragmatic significance in their lives, significance completely outside any Freudian interpretations. Their dreams are messages, omens, indications, promises. For them, dreams are just as real as planting crops, constructing houses, having children, writing songs, or anything else in their lives. Dreams influence their decision making and their way of life. They find in them a feeling of continuity and a realm of volitive and pragmatic action that people of Western cultures cannot even imagine. This describes the dreaming life of the Huicholes in general. In the dreams of a marakame (shaman), we will find even more surprising possibilities, very close to the experiences Castaneda relates.

And, what is most incredible: the dream experience of the Huichole, and the Freudian dream, and even the possibilities of dreams of the second attention or *dreaming* are, in fact, universal possibilities.

So, if it is true that in our society we only know Freudian dreams, it is also true that they are not our only possibility. There exist other ways to dream. Ways that open the door to unusual experiences. Ways that lead to the second attention, power, and awareness of the other self. We can learn these other ways. We can learn to set up *dreaming*.

DREAMING: THE NOT-DOING OF DREAMS

As related to us by Castaneda, one of the two great areas of practice (the other is stalking) among the warriors of the nagual's party involves working in the realm of dreams. Don Juan refers to working with dreams as one of the avenues to power and grants it fundamental importance within his system of knowledge. In his system, *dreaming* denotes a dream that is experienced without completely losing consciousness, and it begins the moment you realize you are dreaming.

Besides referring to the art of *dreaming* as it is presented in the works of Castaneda, I will also mention some aspects that come into focus when we ourselves begin to practice, with some success, the specific techniques we find in them.

Setting up *dreaming* begins with what seems like a very simple technique (III-114): we must dream we are looking at our hands. So simple. Before going to sleep, we give ourselves the order to find our hands in our dreams. It is, however, not as simple as it appears when we experience it first hand and confront it in all its magnitude. Anyone who has achieved this knows what I am talking about: when we find our hands in dreams, the sensation it gives is very strange and intense. It feels as strange as we would feel if, in this exact moment, the book in our hands or the room we are in were to disappear in front of our very eyes to be replaced by some kind of phantom reality. Naturally, an event like this would cause a high degree of amazement; we would feel excitement at having discovered another world whose existence we had never suspected.

And amazement is precisely what is felt upon finding our hands in our dreams. Nothing less. When our *dreaming bodies* (what Castaneda refers to as the *dreamed*) look at their hands, they are obeying an order that comes from another world. From a world that they did not know existed. The everyday world is the other world for the *dreamed*—and the *dreamed*, as one of the aspects of the awareness of the other self, does not remember or know anything of the *dreamer* or that world. The *dreamed* knows nothing of the tonal, the counterpart as the nagual is the counterpart of the *dreamer*. For the *dreamed*, everyday reality is as inconceivable and unreal as the *dreamed* world is for us.

THE OTHER SELF OF THE OTHER SELF

The fact is that the *dreamed* and the *dreamer* never remember one another. They live in parallel realities—together but separated. We are the other selves for the *dreamed* and our world is their separate reality. Ultimately our rationality makes the world of the *dreamed* a mere fantasy extension of the reality that we know, a world of illusion that has no real existence, or we simply forget what we've dreamed. To truly remember the other would imply that we are indeed the dream of the *dreaming body*. And this is precisely what the *dreaming bodies* do when they look at their hands, they become aware they are *dreaming*, and they remember the *dreamer* and the *dreamer's* world. And with this simple act, they perform an unusual maneuver: they create a point of contact between the two sides of awareness, between worlds that normally never touch, that mutually ignore each other. This is why don Juan speaks of the art of *dreaming* as a bridge to the other self, helping to unite the two sides of awareness, tonal and nagual, into an existential unity that he calls the totality of oneself (IV-270).

The ultimate purpose behind all the work with stalking and *dreaming* is to remember the other self in order to integrate that self into that totality. For don Juan *dreaming* is the best avenue to power because it is the door that leads directly to the nagual, returning us to the unknown and mysterious side of our awareness.

Dreaming is the not-doing of dreams, the reciprocal counterpart of not-doing in the world of everyday affairs. Thus, as stalking allows us to move the assemblage point in order to remember the other self, *dreaming* permits the *dreamed* to move the assemblage point in order to remember the *dreamer*. Both forms of not-doing represent the effort that each side of our awareness must make to remember its other self.

One of the advantages of the not-doing of dreams is that

during sleep the assemblage point moves naturally away from its habitual position. It loosens to the degree of not being so rooted to it usual position—even in ordinary dreams—thus making it easier to move to new and unaccustomed positions.

The ways in which we can use our *dreaming* practically have no limits. In my own experience, using techniques of *dreaming* has meant the possibility for action during the hours most people consider idle time or, at most, for resting.

THE RECIPROCITY OF THE WORLD OF THE *DREAMED*

One of the aspects that makes *dreaming* an area of such usefulness is the reciprocal relationship it has with the world of everyday life: the world of dreams corresponds to the world we know when we are awake. I don't mean that what we dream bears a literal resemblance to what we live. Rather, the type of life we lead results in the kind of dreams we have. Freudian lives result in Freudian dreams. So, it follows that not-doing in everyday life results in the not-doing of dreams: *dreaming*.

What is incredible is how this reciprocity functions. The modification of the way we approach everyday life modifies the way we dream, and the modification of the way we dream can modify our everyday life. The realm of our dreams also becomes an area in which we can work for change and for freedom. This means that we can change aspects of our daily life during dreams. Aspects impossible to change using conventional methods can be modified with the help of the other self—and with the power of the second attention that belongs to that self—simply by focusing our *dreaming* on them.

Finding nonordinary solutions to problems and needs that appear insolvable becomes a concrete possibility when we put into play the power that comes from the "nagual side" of our awareness. By *dreaming* we can modify the course of events or discover new solutions to old problems.

Remember that true creativity comes from the left side of awareness.

Castaneda tells us that the warriors of his group developed and enriched the basic activities of their daily lives through *dreaming* (VI-54). Pablito, as a carpenter, learned how to build things; Nestor, who sold medicinal plants, found ways of curing the sick; and Benigno, who had an oracle, found solutions for peoples' problems. Thus, persons with tasks that they consider to be truly their own will find in *dreaming* fertile soil for the harvesting of secrets that will enrich them.

Finding lost objects or missing persons, curing illnesses, or deciding on a course of action, are a few examples of what can be achieved through the not-doing of normal dreaming, to say nothing of the fun and marvel of witnessing incredible worlds through the vehicle of the *dreaming body*. In *dreaming*, it is possible to focus on things of this world as well as of the other.

A HIDDEN TREASURE IN THE OTHER SELF

When we achieve a state of controlled awareness during dreaming, we not only endow our *dreaming body* with the possibility of acting deliberately and pragmatically, but also our everyday self begins to see life and itself from a new perspective.

I would like to add, by way of example, a commentary about my first experience with finding my hands in my dreams. I was studying for a career in anthropology at the time. Spurred on by having read the books by Castaneda, I spent some time trying to remember to look for my hands while dreaming but without success. One night, however, I had a dream that at first didn't seem to be anything special. I found myself on the roof of an enormous castle. There was a door that opened onto a winding spiral staircase descending down through the tower. I entered and began to descend. Everything, walls and steps, was made of dark gray stone.

There was very little light. I kept descending, spurred on by a curiosity that became more and more urgent. There were no windows to permit me to see beyond the thick curving walls. Down and down I went, endlessly it seemed, until I had the feeling I was far below ground level of the castle, in the basement level or maybe lower. My sensation of urgency became a certainty: I knew that down there below, if I arrived, something completely new and unknown was waiting for me, something that would have a great impact on my life. Finally I arrived at the bottom. I opened a heavy door and found myself in a completely empty stone room with enormous windows on the opposite wall and the side walls. These consisted of rectangular openings in the thick walls, without glass or window frames, and their size was such that they took up the greater part of the wall. Through these three large windows the only things visible were the sea, the horizon, and the blue sky. The turquoise blue of the sea produced in me a deep sense of melancholy. I felt incomplete. Something was missing in my life and whatever it was lay out there in that deep blue. It was like the call of a world that I had not seen but could intuit. I felt this very clearly and this clarity was yearning and melancholy. Tears ran down my face and I realized suddenly: I'm dreaming! This is a dream. My hands! I have to look at my hands! I tried to lift my hands and they seemed very heavy. Through great effort I managed to lift them and then I remembered the other world, the man who was sleeping. The dream image began to change; the sensation that something unusual was about to occur overwhelmed me. The whole scene around me, which until then had appeared natural, suddenly became strange and ghostlike. I knew the walls and the whole scene would vanish at any moment, that their existence depended on my will to keep them there, although I did not know how to do it. I saw the walls tremble as though they were an image from a movie projector. I returned to my hands and found the fingers disappearing momentarily. After a moment I decided to take action and make use of the situation, occupying myself with a matter of some importance in my life. . . .

I woke up the next day and began my daily activities. The sadness and melancholy of my dream were still with me. Only, this sadness contained at the very bottom a flavor of secret happiness. It was like having a treasure. I had discovered a new world—a world in which to look and act, in which I could find secrets and from which I could reap benefits. What mysteries did it offer? Did it have limits?

Late afternoon found me in the classroom at the school of anthropology. They were discussing sociological and anthropological theories. And I, normally an active student, saw everything as from a distance. The world of intellectual discussions and self-importance seemed to me so barren. What did they know of my dream? Of what importance was all this in comparison to the excitement of discovering a new world? No one knew it, but I was happy. I felt I possessed a secret treasure. I was flooded with the happiness and melancholy of having glimpsed the other self. I knew that after that day, my life would never again be the same.

Some general remarks about the technique

In general terms, a dream using the second attention—in other words *dreaming*—involves achieving control over the general situation of a dream. In contrast to ordinary dreams, we can act deliberately or even with premeditation. This type of dream begins with the awareness that we are dreaming. Realizing we are living a dream incorporates into the experience an extraordinary awareness that permits the *dreamer* to use that dream pragmatically.

Dreaming requires a special form of attention known as the second attention, a term referring to the generally unknown capacity of awareness to give order to the reality encountered beyond the ordinary description of the world. The first attention aids in putting in order and sustaining perception of right-side awareness. The second attention gives order to the perception of left-side awareness, which takes place in *dreaming*. The second attention, since it is not something familiar, must be learned and developed. In the case of dreams, this means developing the ability to sustain the vision of the dream, giving it continuity and congruence it normally lacks. Not-doing while *dreaming* entails learning to perceive as we do naturally in our everyday world. While the problem in daily life is learning to transform a reality we generally regard as fixed and immutable, in *dreaming* there is presented the opposite problem of sustaining a reality that normally is constantly changing. A special form of attention is required to maintain in focus the contents of a dream and thus achieve a functional order amongst the chaos so characteristic of ordinary dreams. By this I mean we cannot stare fixedly at a dream image without it transforming into something else.

It is interesting to note that left-side awareness is like the reality in the mirror: reciprocal but opposite. In ordinary reality we must strive to use peripheral vision to achieve inner silence and to perceive reality as a whole rather than as fragmented and contradictory. In the reality of dreams, what is required is the ability to focus, to sustain the vision instead of using the peripheral vision normally used on that side of awareness. The doing on one side of awareness becomes a not-doing on the other. Both can be used to create points of contact between the two sides to gradually integrate both sides of awareness into a single unity.

And finally, the practice of *dreaming* aids in the development of what is known in the work of don Carlos as the *dreaming body*. This begins to take place the moment the practice of *dreaming* acquires a continuity that makes it functionally useful for the handling of everyday affairs. The development of the *dreaming body* is cumulative: the more we involve ourselves in dreaming, the more concretion and efficiency it gives to our dreams. We are learning to sustain new positions of the assemblage point that correspond to *dreaming*.

TECHNIQUES

Rather than a group of techniques for achieving *dreaming*, Castaneda's work puts forth a series of tasks to perform once *dreaming* awareness has been attained, although there are no specific steps for arriving at said awareness. This is natural since this awareness has to do with an unaccustomed movement of the assemblage point. Any specific instructions may or may not be appropriate depending on our specific situation (our particular "doings").

First I will present the different steps we must carry out in order to consolidate awareness of the *dreaming body*. Later I will go into detail on the techniques (which in reality are aids to bring our awareness to remember the other self during *dreaming*). There really is no way to say how to do it; what happens is that in a given moment our body simply does it—it remembers.

58. FINDING YOUR HANDS

Everything begins with remembering the other self. At a given moment, you as the *dreamed* simply remember to carry out some task such as looking at your hands. The specific item chosen is not important; what matters is to give yourself the order while awake and carry it out while *dreaming*. As the *dreamed* remembers, you perceive the order coming from somewhere and then you remember the other world. You remember the *dreamer*. From this point, *dreaming* begins and all the tasks you must complete can now be carried out.

Using the hands is often the best choice since they are always there and there will be no trouble finding them. But anything you find, any object, your feet or any other part of the body, can serve as well. The trick is to remember the order and carry it out.

In spite of its seeming simplicity, the first step is usually the most difficult. In courses and conferences I often encounter people who have practiced for years, giving themselves the order to find their hands but without success. These people always ask me the same questions: "What is happening? Why can't I find my hands? How do you do it?" What happens is that in the world of *dreaming*, a reciprocal of the world of everyday life, the practice of not-doing requires a loosening of structured "doings". Thus, if you insist on maintaining the fixed and mechanically repetitive practice of "doing" in everyday life, it will be practically impossible to develop the necessary freedom to practice *dreaming*. The reverse is also true; practicing the not-doing of *dreaming* prepares you for not-doing in ordinary life. Therefore, what is needed is coordinated effort on the part of both the *dreamer* and the *dreamed* in the practice of not-doing.

This was easily observed among those who shared in workshops in the field, especially those who stayed the most days—they simply started finding their hands in their dreams. There was a reason for this: during these workshops, the participants were removed from their world and daily activities and instead were immersed day and night in the practice of not-doing. From this observation, we derived a strategy for action: If you want to find your hands in your dreams, besides giving yourself the order to do so, you must also saturate your body with not-doing during the day.

The general procedure would consist of spending the whole day in activities that are totally out of the ordinary. Particularly effective results are obtained if these activities are in no way flattering to the ego, such as spending an entire weekend working close to people and performing actions that are completely opposed to your way of being; or carrying out tasks you don't like, tasks that require a great mental and physical effort, and at which you are particularly clumsy. If as a result you become the target of criticism by people around you, so much the better. Treating the ego in this way tends to shrink the tonal and therefore is very useful in setting up *dreaming*. Naturally, you must use common sense in choosing a suitable strategy so as not to put yourself in dangerous situations that could cause real damage, those that go beyond simply giving the ego a hard time.

Any of the exercises of attention, not-doing, or stopping the internal dialogue that appear in this book are appropriate for setting up *dreaming*.

Once you find your hands for the first time, it gradually becomes easier. Each time you practice the not-doing of dreams, your body is filling itself with the cumulative effect of not-doing, which serves as raw material for further *dreaming* experiences.

60. SUSTAINING DREAM IMAGES

I have already stated briefly that the base upon which *dreaming* is developed is the capacity to sustain dream images. This is the first task we must carry out once we have remembered the other self and have looked at our hands.

The technique consists of focusing directly on objects in the scene in which you find yourself, beginning with your hands. You will find it is difficult to keep them in focus or even to lift them to eye level; they may be very heavy or they may disappear when you look at them directly. But you also may discover the faculty, the will, that will allow you to sustain the image. You must apply your will to keep the image from disappearing. Fortunately, there is a procedure to make things easier. The *dreamer* need only shift his or her gaze to other objects in the dreaming scene when the first one begins to fade or change. So, from your hands, you look next at any other object; when it begins to change, return to your hands, then back to the object and so on. Little by little begin to take in more objects until you are able to sustain the entire dream image. Once you have learned to do this, the trick is to confine yourself to momentary glances, taking in the entire scene rather than stopping to focus indefinitely on a single object. In this way the scene remains and the dream world acquires continuity.

61. LEARNING TO MOVE

Next you learn how to move. Moving in *dreaming* requires a period of training. It has nothing to do with movement such as is experienced in ordinary dreams, which is done mechanically without any intention on your part. The initial tendency is to try to move as you do in everyday life, only to find it impossible since you lack the solidity of the physical body—the basic reference point for movement. Without that solid feeling and not knowing what you are made of, you often don't know how to begin moving.

Again that word of subtle and mysterious context—the will—comes into play. In *dreaming* you use your will to move. The will has more to do with a feeling or a certainty than with thought. This feeling is generated from slightly below the umbilical region. From there arises the sensation. With practice, you learn to move naturally, although at the beginning there may be a few falls.

62. SPACE AND TIME

The next phase relates to controlling the coordinates, space and time, of your trip—where the dream takes place and in what specific moment.

To begin, choose the place you wish to go while *dreaming*. This can be accomplished in two ways: either begin your *dreaming* in the chosen place, or, starting from a *dreaming* state, then move to where you wish to be. The first is recommended over the second since the second takes more time and requires a high degree of control of movement as well as a good sense of location.

Known places are much more appropriate to start with, those in which everyday life activities take place and especially those in which you feel most comfortable. To reach them during *dreaming*, concentrate attention on them during the day. However, don't concentrate on the entire place; instead center attention on one specific object and later use that object as a guide to "pull" the *dreaming body*.

Observing the object in question for a few hours ought to be sufficient, during which time you should have experienced a few moments of inner silence, moments in which the vision of the object can be converted into a true *dreaming* command. Once you are *dreaming*, simply remember the object and allow the *dreaming body* to be pulled by the attention placed on it.

As to the question of time, there is not much to go on. Begin by choosing to *dream* the selected place either during the day or at night. If you achieve that, the next step is to choose to do *dreaming* at the exact hour in which you are asleep and *dreaming*. This is the fine point of controlling the time of *dreaming*: making that time coincide with the time of the external events of the everyday world.

Practice this by going to sleep at the precise hour in which you wish to act in the chosen place with the *dreaming body*. A morning or evening nap could very well be used for this exercise.

When you can make the time and space of *dreaming* coincide with that of everyday affairs, you are ready to begin to influence your daily life using your *dreaming body*.

63. FINDING YOURSELF

Finally we come to the true test of fire that tells you the *dreamer* if you are truly *dreaming*: a face to face encounter between the *dreamer* and the *dreamed*.

When you are capable of controlling the time and place of your *dreaming*, you can verify directly whether your *dreaming* is taking place during the same time as your everyday world: have an encounter with your physical body asleep in bed. The task now consists of looking for yourself. You the *dreamed* know that someone is *dreaming* you and now you have to have the fortitude and control to find out who is doing the *dreaming*. If you find the *dreamer*, instead of being frightened or waking up, the *dreamer* knows the moment of power has arrived and instead makes use of the experience to achieve the impossible: to influence your everyday world using your *dreaming body*.

Finding yourself asleep can be even more difficult than finding your hands. At least it was for me.

I had been working with my dreams for some time. I was already capable of realizing that I was *dreaming*, of looking at my hands, and had learned how to move. On many occasions, I gave myself the task of looking for my body asleep. Generally I found it difficult to find my house or the place in which I was asleep. Something always got in my way. On some occasions I would arrive at my house only to have something frightening happen just before I entered my bedroom, which would transform my *dreaming* into a nightmare. At one point I realized that there was one constant factor in each one of my failures—fear. Each time my *dreamed* was about to encounter my *dreamer*, I entered into a state of uncontrollable fear. I had no idea why I was so fearful, but once I identified what the trouble was, I decided to face it. I had to go ahead in spite of the fear that barred my way. Finally I was able to enter my room while *dreaming*. Yes, it was my room; all my personal effects were there, all the details were in place, my companion was also there sleeping, and next to her there was someone else—me. In that moment I discovered why I had been so fearful: to discover for certain that it was all real.

That's how it was. All these practices of *dreaming*, while very attractive to me, were at the same time very menacing to my ego, my vision of the world, and the meaning of reality and normality. Even though I had spent much time exploring the possibilities of *dreaming*, up to that point the whole matter had been nothing more than a kind of game I had played with myself. My reason, my ordinary vision of reality had taken refuge—without my knowing it—in the possibility that perhaps all of this business of *dreaming* was just my imagination or a fantasy. That kind of thinking came to an abrupt end in the encounter between my *dreamer* and my *dreamed*. There was nowhere to go. It was true after all. The other self and the other world really existed. It was true that both worlds could come into contact. There was nothing to do but accept this terrifying, but at the same time marvelous, fact. So that's what I did—I accepted the marvel and the terror.

When you finally accept something so incredible and hair-raising as the existence of the *dreaming body* or double, what follows then is action. Leave questions and fears to one side and make use of the situation pragmatically. There are many applications as we shall see shortly.

THE DOUBLE: IS IT DOUBLE OR TRIPLE?

Before going on to the next section, there is one more thing to say regarding the double. In reality, it is not a double but a triple.

The discovery of the triple occurred one night during a very simple dream. I was exchanging jokes with three friends. We were sitting on the floor with our legs crossed. I was seized with an attack of laughter, and suddenly I realized I was *dreaming*. I had that peculiar sensation that is experienced when one starts *dreaming*. Only this time what happened afterward was different. I found myself looking at the scene from the outside, watching myself laughing with my friends. But if I was there laughing, who was doing the looking? Upon asking myself the question, I perceived my own person looking at the scene at the same time I found myself within it. I found myself in two places at once. In that instant something jerked me back to the scene. I found myself again with my friends and to my left a short distance away someone was looking at me with an expression of surprise on his face. It was me! Seeing myself caused me to return to my position as spectator. Then I found myself absorbed in a series of experiments in which I would jump from one perspective to the other, looking at myself from either inside or outside the scene. But that's not all. I found I could split my perception and be in both places at once. While engaged in this, I suddenly realized something else. If this is all a dream and in it there are two people who are "I", who then is *dreaming* us? Upon asking that question, I sensed my physical body asleep. I shifted position in bed and was at the point of waking up, but I managed to retain the control necessary to remain asleep and prolong the experience. From this moment, I was capable of perceiving from the self that was asleep in bed, from the self that was observing the scene of my friends laughing, and from the self that was involved in the scene, jumping from one perception to another. Or I would split my attention and perceive simultaneously from all three points in a process of perception that words cannot adequately describe.

This experience does not contradict the indications of don Juan or don Carlos regarding the double, for in reality the triple is merely one aspect of the *dreaming body* that has to do with its capacity to perceive from the outside or from the inside. We can look at the scene as though we were watching a movie, or we can perceive from inside the scene. And we have the power to choose. The ability to watch the scene from outside is especially useful if the content of the dream is very intense, or even painful. This change from inside to outside allows us a more sober vantage point from which to view the events that take place in *dreaming*.

Commentary on applying dreaming practices

From the moment the *dreamer* encounters his or her physical body asleep, he or she can then begin to make a more pragmatic use of *dreaming*. From the outset it must be stressed that at no time is the physical body to be awakened.

Castaneda indicates that to do so would mean death! In any case, there is no need to experiment—there are more useful things to do:

We can relive problematic scenes from daily life, discover how the *dreaming body* would resolve them, and later apply these solutions to everyday life.

We can develop creative abilities in any personal activities we are involved in—painting, writing, healing, singing, dancing, constructing, and so forth. Creativity knows no limits in the world of the nagual.

We can ascertain facts about people, or about ourselves while observing from the *dreaming* state. In the case of self-observation, however, choose a *dreaming* time frame distinct from the time when you lie down to do your *dreaming*. You will not learn very much trying to observe yourself while asleep.

We can realize things that we desire in our everyday existence during *dreaming*. If we have sufficient energy, the events of our *dreaming* can become the directing force of the events in our everyday life.

Deciding which path to take when at a crossroads in life can be best handled from the totality of the *dreaming* state, within which there is an increased integration between both sides of awareness. We can explore, while *dreaming*, a particular path and find out whether it yields the desired result or not.

Forgiving, letting go of resentment, and approaching other human beings, are just some of the many things that can be done with *dreaming*, providing we have the control to locate the person in question in our *dreaming*. Naturally, approaching anyone this way should be done in a sober and disinterested manner. Any desire to use this power to damage or abuse another would be highly self-destructive. It would not agree with the way of the warrior who—unlike black magicians—can never look upon fellow human beings with intent of harming them, using them, or obtaining personal gratification.

Sharing the *dreaming* experience with someone else requires that both persons should be able to control the time and place of their *dreaming*, should know each other well, and should be familiar to a high degree with one another's energy and tonality. Games, such as using the *dreaming body* to pull the feet of a *dreaming* companion, are permissible only as a means of corroborating the dreaming experience and as long as they do not get out of control.

The exploration of the other world is perhaps the most important application of the work of don Carlos, and it is, of course, a possibility for anyone who penetrates the intricate pathways of *dreaming*. In any case, we should know that to focus the power of *dreaming* on the everyday world requires the sobriety and austerity of the way of the warrior in order to not fall into excesses that could be counterproductive.

64. SOME SUGGESTIONS OF A TECHNICAL NATURE

All along in the work of don Carlos, we find suggestions of a technical nature whose purpose is to achieve better conditions for the exercise of dreaming.

I do not consider it necessary to comply with all of them, since, as I have discovered, a given set of specific procedures can never become habitual in learning to do *dreaming*. Nevertheless, any of those following can be selected according to which ones suit you best. Anyone wishing to know more about them can consult directly the works of Castaneda.

- Upon going to sleep, concentrate on the tip of the sternum—the point from which arises the attention necessary for *dreaming* (VI-135).

- Sleep with a cap or headband around your head, preferably one that has been found while *dreaming*, then located in the physical reality of everyday life (III-147).

- Sleep sitting up, women with their legs crossed and men

with their legs stretched out; sleeping this way inside an elongated cradle would be ideal (VI-137).

• Choose the best time for *dreaming*; in the initial stages this is during the early morning hours when most people are asleep and the force of their attention is at its weakest. This gives greater freedom of action (VI-138).

• Avoid wide flat areas such as a treeless valley, large lakes, or the ocean for doing *dreaming*. Closed-in areas such as caves, hollows, dry riverbeds, or simply a closed room are much better (VI-249).

• Fix your attention by practicing a ritual. Or the monotonous repetition of words or movements, as long as they are devoid of any symbolic content, can be effective for concentrating the attention required for *dreaming* (VI-249).

• Massage the calves of your legs since this part of the body plays an important role in *dreaming* (VI-255).

65. THE OBSERVATION OF *DREAMING* OBJECTS

One technique that merits closer examination is the observation of *dreaming* objects. This is useful in exercising the second attention, which is required to transform an ordinary dream into *dreaming*. Castaneda goes into this in detail in *The Second Ring of Power* (V-284–289). It consists of the following elements.

In a seated and relaxed position, focus your attention for hours on a specific object, all the while making an effort to maintain a state of inner silence. Later, during *dreaming*, try to find the object. Once it is found, proceed to influence said object from the *dreaming* state. The suggested steps for this are:

1. Observe a dry leaf. Get to know even the smallest details of a given leaf to the point where—relying on memory alone—you are able to tell the difference between this dry leaf and any other. Do the exercise for several days, each day with a different leaf. During *dreaming*, try to find the observed leaf.

2. Gaze at a pile of dry leaves and trace spiral movements with one finger. Observe the detail of the figures and designs that form; later find these same designs in *dreaming*.

3. Make designs in the dry leaves while *dreaming*, then look for these same designs to form themselves in the pile of leaves you are observing while awake.

4. Go on to observing other things such as small plants, trees, insects, rocks, rain, fog, and clouds in that order.

This exercise is not only for acquiring the ability to find the observed object during *dreaming* but also to cultivate the second attention. This makes it a very appropriate exercise to aid in finding your hands in *dreaming*.

For a more detailed review of the specific techniques used in *dreaming*, as described by don Carlos in his works, consult the glossary of techniques found at the end of this book.

NINE

THE BODY AS AWARENESS

CORPORAL PERCEPTION

The first truth of the mastery of awareness according to Castaneda is that human beings are part of and suspended within the eagle's emanations (VII-49). This truth in particular alludes to the fact that we are luminous beings—specific presences located in a universe made up of fields of energy that don Juan calls the eagle's emanations.

The portion of energy that we are is contained during our lives in a form or mold known as the human form (VII-280). The essential characteristic of that field of energy is the ability to perceive, which is why don Juan tells Carlos that "we are a feeling, an awareness encased here . . ." at which point he lightly taps his chest (IV-18).

In speaking of our natural ability as perceivers, we are not referring to the ego—which is a "verbalizer" not a perceiver—but rather to the body as a field of energy. Therefore, there is no point in trying to determine which parts of the body perceive. The entire luminous cocoon perceives.

Corporal perception takes place with the totality of the body, even the part that lies beyond the boundaries of the skin. According to seers, perceiving this way makes us look like large luminous eggs (II-29). Corporal perception can be thought of as the opposite of ordinary everyday perception, which is nothing more than a combination of the dictates of the ego, personal history, and the work of the five senses. Corporal perception, on the other hand, is direct and allows no interpretations. In this context, the body/mind connection loses its meaning since the body becomes part of the total field of energy and the process of perception involves the interaction between the energy of the luminous egg and the fields of energy outside it.

From the beginning of their relationship, don Juan insists that Carlos pay more attention to his feelings and forget thinking. He tells Carlos that, while the mind needs to learn, the body simply knows. The content of everything don Juan teaches contains a corporal dimension that is rooted in action, not thoughts or words. A warrior always acts first before philosophizing. The knowledge of the body represents a departure from the usual Western notions about what constitutes knowledge, in which it is usually associated with the capacity to formulate verbal or mental enunciations that supposedly reveal the characteristics of a thing or a known process.

Western notions of what constitutes perception are also limited. People are accustomed to treating it as something accomplished exclusively by our five senses—particularly sight—which report on everything perceived to the thought center that we feel is located behind our eyes. Don Juan proposes that we can use our senses in ways outside the ordinary, that we can comprehend the nature of things without having to think about it, that the body has within itself silent knowledge and its own memory.

Corporal perception as referred to in the works of don Carlos is a silent knowledge that has nothing to do with words or thoughts. Rather it implies a direct interaction between the body and the world.

In the various walks of attention, and in many other exercises, there is reference to the need to place our attention on what the body feels. In this way, we move ourselves into the realm of corporal perception. The aforementioned examples of the children who are trained to read without using their eyes or of a body well trained in the gait of power are just some illustrations of the body's capacity to perceive in unusual ways.

TECHNIQUES

The majority of techniques taught to Carlos by don Juan imply the use of corporal perception as a necessary element since there exists no perception other than corporal. Thus, the purpose of the following section is to present some techniques that put an emphasis on the relation between the body and the world, especially the world of nature where there is no place for rational thinking.

66. THE WALK OF THE MIDPOINT

The first thing required is to locate with mathematical precision the exact midpoint of the body (VII-125). Measure it right to the millimeter to find the exact midpoint in both length and width. Once found it can be marked with ink or by placing a small pebble on the spot, taping it in place or using a type of glue that will not damage the skin.

Locating this point is useful not only for this technique but for many others as well since centering attention on it will permit a more heightened perception in any situation.

With the midpoint located and marked, begin the walk. Generally speaking, it consists of the same elements as those indicated for the walk of attention, only in this case your attention will be centered on three principal aspects: the midpoint, the breathing, and the surroundings.

Breathing plays the role of helping to achieve rhythm and

concentration while walking. Attention on the surroundings is intuitive, not visual. Your eyes should "sweep" the ground directly in front of your feet; thus it would be helpful to have some kind of guidance, such as doing it in a group Indian file or, if alone, over known terrain.

The key to this exercise is to locate perception and awareness in your midpoint, sensing that place as though it were the root of your perception. Take long walks to practice perceiving a variety of different surroundings, feeling the distinct nature of each place without the use of your eyes. This does not imply trying to imagine visually what the surroundings look like. Rather it involves directly sensing how each place affects your energy and feelings.

The pebble taped to your midpoint, by the way, can also be used as an aid in setting up *dreaming*; simply sleep with it in place.

67. THE BED OF STRINGS (III-162)

This exercise could qualify as one of the most pleasant, but not because it yields pleasure similar to what is ordinarily understood as such. The pleasure it gives has to do directly with a profound sense of well-being, which arises from the beneficial effect on the field of energy. It functions as an energy restorer, providing the deep rest needed for recovery after a difficult or especially exhausting experience. We have used it for recovering sobriety and for comfort after cathartic experiences.

The technique as presented by Castaneda in *Journey to Ixtlan* requires two people, one to make the bed and one to use it. The exercise is done on top of a small hill and includes the following steps:

1. Find an appropriate spot to make the bed, using the method of sensing it with the eyes. That can be done either by crossing them or simply by sweeping your gaze over the surroundings.

2. Take some dry leaves found near the site and lay them in a circle large enough for a person to lie down in.

3. Sweep the area within the circle using a branch but without actually touching the ground.

4. Pick up all the rocks found within the circle and classify them into two groups according to size.

5. Place the small rocks symmetrically and equidistant in a circle directly on top of the circle of leaves, pressing them down so they are well seated.

6. Standing on top of the hill, the person making the bed begins rolling the larger rocks downhill, one by one, while the person who will use the bed receives them below, taking care not to confuse them with any other rocks that might be displaced. As they arrive at the bottom, that person places the rocks in a circle as was done at the top of the hill, until the circle is complete to the last rock.

7. The assistant above cushions the upper circle with small twigs, filling it completely, while the person below ascends the hill.

8. The one who will use the bed places some leaves, given by the assistant, over the abdominal region, and lies down inside the rock circle to rest or sleep for however long he or she feels is necessary.

The way this technique is practiced in my work groups varies in some of the details from the way it is described here, but it has given magnificent results regardless. In this procedure as well as similar ones, the results obtained rely both on the techniques used and on the personal power of the one carrying out the exercise. In the case of Carlos that person was don Juan. In this exercise, as in many others, we have used the warrior's way, as expressed by don Juan: "A warrior is impeccable when he trusts his personal power whether it be small or enormous . . ." (III-183).

The variation we have practiced includes the following:

- It requires a state of heightened sensitivity and awareness reached through any kind of appropriate practice.

- It is to be done out in the country, preferably in a pine woods, either in flatlands or mountainous areas.

- The two people required will use the bed—constructed by both of them—alternately between them.
- Begin by looking for rocks to make the circle. To receive the full benefit of the exercise, it is important that this be carried out with the utmost concentration, in complete silence, and with rocks more or less uniform in size and shape and as round as possible. The location of the rocks, and the individual characteristics of each rock, must be observed with great care, since at the end of the exercise they will have to be returned to their original places.
- With the rocks, make a circle big enough for one person to lie down with arms extended to the sides and legs slightly open and extended as well. The construction of the circle also must be done in a state of maximum concentration, working for a perfect circle with an exactly equal distance between each rock.
- Next gather small branches, leaves, and flowers to cushion the area inside the circle of rocks. It is important not only to concentrate while doing this, but also to remember your relationship with the plants, bushes, and flowers at the moment you pick them. Remember that in the same unexpected and definitive way your own lives will be cut off to serve as food or assistance to something or someone else. Besides asking the pardon of each plant, flower, or bush that is cut, remember to use no more than those necessary for the purpose, filling out the bed with dry leaves, if needed.
- When everything has been gathered, cushion the inside of the circle, placing the materials so as to make the bed not only comfortable but aesthetically pleasing as well. As always, the more care, concentration, and goodwill put into the task, the better will be the result.
- If the air is somewhat cold, place a few leaves under the clothes just below the umbilical region of the person using the bed.
- With all the preparations out of the way, decide who will rest first and who will be the assistant. The assistant removes the other's shoes, then with an embrace lays the

other person down inside the circle face up with arms and legs open and fully extended. If you are resting, close your eyes and—if desired—change position to find the one most comfortable. Remain there as long as necessary, whether it be a few minutes or several hours.

• Once you are sufficiently rested, change places. The one who rested now becomes the assistant, following the same steps as the other did.

• When both of you are finished, all the rocks are put back where they were found and the leaves, flowers, and branches are scattered in such a way as to leave the smallest possible trace of your presence.

Commentary on the technique

Two elements have to be taken into account when doing this technique. The first is that it is used after practices or exercises that have left us in a state of heightened sensitivity and we feel the need for some kind of support such as the rest afforded by the bed of strings. And second, damaging nature is something a warrior will permit only for very specific purposes. This exercise is not simply for resting or "to see what it feels like." If done inappropriately, the plants, flowers, and surrounding nature could turn against us, making us ill instead of healing us. If we merely wish to rest, a simple pile of dry leaves will do nicely.

EXERCISES WITHOUT SEEING

In the chapter on stopping the internal dialogue I referred superficially to the practice of using a blindfold (see exercise 43). A more detailed version is one of the exercises most representative of Corporal Perception. This one and those that follow fall into the category of what I have called "exercises of the blind".

In these exercises, we are the blind persons. Instead of reducing our activities in fear of not being able to see, we increase them. This makes possible the emergence of a form of attention that will permit us to experience our other four senses in an especially intense and unaccustomed way. Even more important, it allows the body to remember little by little. The body can function as a perceiver in ways that will not necessarily agree with what we consider to be the ordinary way to perceive through the senses.

The trick is to be ready to forget the world the way we are accustomed to perceiving it with our eyes. Most people, while temporarily blindfolded, try to visualize their surroundings through imagination and memory. Here it is best to forget our eyes and what they have told us about the world in order to penetrate into a world without light, in which we are transformed into a being of the darkness, where we feel completely natural. In place of being concerned about the absence of light, we learn to know, to act in, and to enjoy the world of darkness.

This means discovering that fear and archaic rejection of darkness are but prejudice that we can do away with. As in the natural world of day and night, light and shadow, in our own being we find corresponding ontological variability. Thus, if we accept darkness as a natural condition, we give ourselves the possibility of adjusting to it, of coming into contact with our "being of darkness" that has nothing to do with the usual absurd association between darkness and evil.

Realize that the objects around us are not going to disappear simply because we can no longer see them—they will be transformed into what these same objects are in darkness. This is a point to consider very seriously: the world is not the same in darkness, nor are we ourselves. The sorcerer knows this and therefore takes a special interest in this fact. He or she knows that during darkness the natural transformation of the world and all beings into shadows readily facilitates the penetration into nonordinary reality just as our ordinary description of reality and its flow of habitual perceptions weakens it.

68. EXERCISE OF THE BLIND

The exercise begins with the very simple act of covering your eyes with a bandanna or some type of cloth to prevent all light from entering your eyes. It may be necessary to use several layers of tissue paper over each eye underneath the blindfold to assure complete darkness.

Now that you are "blind" (see exercise 43) you must remain active, trying to accustom yourself to the new situation.

In many cases the presence of someone to assist can be very useful and even indispensable, someone who will accompany you, keeping you out of dangerous situations during difficult exercises or when any other problem crops up. The assistant should speak as little as possible in order not to disturb your process of sensitization. At the same time, he or she should avoid "overprotecting" you so that you can become self-sufficient in the least possible time. The assistant will also help to create the situations required by each exercise, such as guiding you when you are not in condition to orient yourself.

Where walking or running is involved, you should lift your knees higher than normal, almost like marching, especially over irregular terrain. This way you will be better able to adapt to variations in the terrain or to obstacles such as rocks or tree trunks. Another appropriate technique would be jump-trotting, lifting the thighs on each step. One thigh is lifted immediately after the other while maintaining the necessary flexibility so that the legs can adapt themselves to any variation in the terrain. In areas with many trees or other large obstacles, extending a hand in front of your face may prevent injury, especially when doing this without someone to assist.

The following exercises can be practiced on different occasions according to their grade of difficulty and to the grade of proficiency and knowledge you are developing about your being of darkness.

69. THE HOME OF THE BLIND

This exercise consists of remaining at home blindfolded all day, carrying out all of the ordinary activities that can be done without putting yourself in danger—sweeping the floor, getting dressed, drawing, writing, listening to music, doing exercise. Cooking can be done as long as extreme caution is taken with the stove, especially a gas stove. At the end of the day, go to bed leaving the blindfold on until dawn of the following day. The presence of someone to assist is recommended.

70. THE WALK OF THE BLIND

At the beginning you will take only a simple uncomplicated excursion. It requires the company of a guide who will help keep you out of danger and who will serve as a "blind person's guide" during the walk. The guide walks in front of you and you lay your hand on the guide's left shoulder for orientation while you walk. It should be remembered that touching the shoulder serves only for purposes of orientation, not for support, so avoid the urge to use the guide as a "human walking stick." The longer the walk, the greater will be the results. As you gain expertise, take more complicated excursions, such as climbing a mountain or walking over irregular terrain. A variation of this would be the blind Indian file in which the same procedure is followed but with more than two participants, each touching the left shoulder of the one in front. Two guides would be best for this, one at the head and one at the rear to prevent any mishaps.

71. THE CALL

In this exercise you will remain where you are placed by an assistant who then moves to another area some distance away. The assistant will call you using a particular sound that you have agreed on beforehand. The distance between you may vary a great deal depending on the type of terrain and your ability. It could be anywhere from a few yards to thousands of yards. When you hear the call, begin walking toward the sound until you encounter the assistant, guided only by your ears and the sensitivity of your body. This first step completed, you remain there while the assistant moves to a new place to repeat the exercise. Do it as many times as desired. The technique of lifting the knees is very useful in this case. The assistant should be very careful to note if there are any serious obstacles such as holes, large rocks, or steep descents that might be dangerous to the "blind person."

72. RACE TO THE UNKNOWN

This is one of my favorite exercises because it allows us to penetrate in a more direct and profound way into the experience of corporal perception and aids in the emergence of our being of darkness. It requires the presence at least two assistants with the necessary strength and ability to serve as effective aides during its execution. The race to the unknown consists of running at top speed between two previously chosen points while blindfolded. It should be done over flat ground, either bare or grass-covered earth. Obstacles that could trip the runner should be avoided—even small ones such as rocks, bushes, or any protuberance in the soil within the area marked off for the exercise as well as in the area immediately surrounding it. It is carried out in the following manner:

1. Determine the starting and finishing points, locating one or more assistants at each point. The distance between these points should not be less than 20 yards or more than 150 yards.

2. Stand on the starting line, blindfold in place, and facing toward the finish line.

3. An assistant at the finish line then yells loudly, "On your mark, get set, go!"

4. Take off at a full run while the assistant at the finish line

continually yells "Over here, over here!" to orient you by ear. If you stray too far from the path, the assistant should yell "To the right!" or "To the left!" or whatever is necessary.

5. When you arrive at the finish line, the assistant yells "Stop!" and with any other assistants physically stops your forward progress, taking care to avoid injury to themselves or to you. The correct way to do this is to take you by the thorax and abdomen with one arm bent as in an embrace and then to move with you a little way so as to cushion the impact. In most cases you will have stopped your forward motion, thus making this process much easier than it would seem.

6. Repeat the exercise as many times as desired until you loosen up completely, allowing yourself to run at top speed.

7. Vary this exercise with a race between two runners, which will require the presence of more assistants, including some placed along the route to prevent collisions between the participants. Each runner will have different assistants who will call out by his or her name to avoid confusion. The arrival points should be separated by at least 12 feet. No more than two people should run at any one time.

Commentary on the techniques

This information applies to those coordinating the exercise. The success of these exercises depends on creating conditions that instill confidence for their physical safety in those participating. Initially the exercise by itself tends to provoke fear and insecurity and participants will tend to run cautiously. But if those participating have sufficient confidence in those who are coordinating the exercise, trusting that all details have been taken care of and that there is no real danger, they are much more likely to "let go," knowing the only obstacle is their own internal fear. Making sure the runner is well taken care of in the first attempts will inspire his or her confidence. For example, if at the moment of hearing "Stop!", the runner is handled with firmness and security but without roughness, he or she will know there is nothing to fear, and the next time can run to the maximum. Also it is important to yell loudly and clearly so that the runner does not feel "lost" at any moment.

As a participant you should lift your knees higher than normal. In the unlikely event that you should trip and fall, simply keep your hands at your sides and roll on the ground while avoiding tension, fright, or abandon. The principal recommendation is to keep moving ahead. This exercise is a true race toward the unknown and—like life in general—it is best to keep going ahead rather than to reverse. Although the initial tendency will be to run with the head and shoulders back, you must learn to run with the body forward, seeking the darkness and penetrating it, not fearing it. Think beforehand that there is no danger, that this exercise deals with accepting the experience of penetrating the unknown as a question of enjoyment and marvel rather than fear or force. In practice, when you can let your body run in darkness, the velocity reached can be greater than if you were not blindfolded. One thing that can help here is—again—to give up clinging to mental visualization. It will not help to run while trying to imagine visually the surroundings; rather it is better to accept the darkness. A frequent comment about this exercise is that it can produce what has been called the "tunnel effect." This refers to the effect produced when you have conquered all fear and have fully accepted the darkness. In that moment the sensation of darkness is experienced like a black tunnel through which you pass with dizzying speed. As though it were riding a toboggan, the body feels pulled onward, with a feeling of enjoyment, euphoria, and intensity that brings you into a state of being and awareness that could very well be called the other self.

TEN

THE WARRIOR'S GREATEST LOVE

THE MODERN WORLD: SOCIETIES WITHOUT LOVE

Loneliness appears to be an inexorable condition of human beings.

For average persons, loneliness is the most immediate expression of the unrealistic relationships that we have established with the world and with other people. We are surrounded by people in great numbers: family, friends, boss, subordinates, neighbors, but nevertheless are alone among them. We have been trained to possess, to use, to compete, to fear, to lie, and to hide, but not to encounter, to communicate, and to love. We arrange everything in order to stay separated.

We are surrounded also by nature with myriad forms and colors, with trees and animals of all types, rivers, oceans, deserts, jungles, lakes, and mountains, a marvelous planet to inhabit, an infinite number of lights in the firmament of which to dream. Yet none of this affects us; we remain alone. We have learned that the world consists of many more or less inert things that were put here for our use. Our entire history appears to be nothing more than the gradual development of our capacity to use and exploit more and more the world of nature.

A worldview such as this implies that we regard ourselves as being separate from nature. In the ancient Judeo-Christian tradition as well as in more recent theories of Marxism or the economic vision of the capitalist world, nature is to be dominated and exploited. Always *homo sapiens* are the possessors of the Earth, their relation with her one of use and exploitation. If this is the way we relate to the being who has given us a body and life, food, home, and beauty, then it follows that we would relate in a similar way to everything else, including other people. This is why a Western adult male is so capable of "possessing" a woman and at the same time so incapable of loving her.

This vocation of arrogance, violence, and avarice characterizes our way of being in these times. The result of so much violence is the tendency toward self-destruction, ranging from suicidal depression—increasingly common in today's society—to the wholesale destruction of the environment, which is surely the suicide of human society. All this in the midst of terrible loneliness.

REMEMBERING THE EARTH

In my encounters with indigenous communities, I have discovered that there are other ways of relating to the Earth and to nature. For a Mexican Indian, the Earth is not of people, but people are of the Earth. Indigenous peoples of Toltec descent speak of corn as *no nacatl* (our flesh), expressing an awareness that the fruits of Earth give us body and existence.

Indigenous Nahuas of our time, here at the end of the millennium, still perform the ceremony of "remembering the Earth," whose real name is a secret shared only by those of us who have had the good fortune to participate in it. In this ceremony the entire community, which normally appears to follow the religious calendar of the Catholic Church, retires to a group of caves known only to them for the celebration of a ritual. This ritual, whose nature I am not permitted to reveal, affords those participating the real possibility of connecting directly with the awareness of the Earth. Not having a fixed date for celebrating this "remembering the Earth" has made it impossible for the local priest, after ten years in the community, to ascertain where and how his parishioners carry out such pagan rites, which he has been trying without success to eradicate. (As far as I know, no other non-Indian has ever participated in this three-day ceremony. Perhaps in another work I will relate the circumstances that led to my being able to participate and what occurred afterward.) After centuries of being dominated and exterminated, the indigenous Mexicans actively maintain their intimate relationship with the entity that has given them being.

This feeling of integration and nonseparation brings the indigenous peoples of Mexico to love the Earth as a conscious living being. The same feeling allowed the pre-Columbian civilizations of America to develop a science and technology that could very well be called ecological. This technology permitted them to develop, for example, large population centers (30 million inhabitants in the central region of the country[17]) without perceptible deterioration of the environment.

THE MESSAGE FROM THE OTHERS

Today, with our unconsciousness at the point of destroying the Earth, to turn our gaze to the indigenous world that knows alternative ways to relate to the world opens possibilities of encountering a message of life that we urgently need to hear. And we need to hear it now. This is a matter of life or death. Now we are at the point of destroying the last vestiges of these ancient civilizations. Now we are at the point of

---

[17] See Woodrow Borah, *El soglo de la depression in Nueva Espana*, Mexico City, 1983.

remaining completely alone after centuries of exterminating the others—the ones who are different.

The thinking of don Juan and his party of warriors is permeated also with this assurance and feeling of closeness to the Earth, with love for the origin. A body of work such as that of don Carlos also serves as messenger, a bridge between that world of magic and mystery and our own world of arrogance and boredom.

The predilection of warriors is simple and clear—the manifestation of the awareness of human beings who know that the Earth is the fundamental provider of everything. It is she who gives them a home, who feeds them, who provides beauty at every step, who is filled with mysteries, each one representing a challenge. The predilection of warriors is to secretly enjoy the warmth of the Earth that envelops them. They are never alone; the Earth accompanies and sustains them in all moments of life. She is that enormous being whose inexhaustible love aids in curing afflictions and sadness, who washes away pettiness. Awareness of the Earth as profound and incommensurable yields power and secrets to warriors when they put forgetfulness and personal history to one side and humbly open their spirit to her sweet presence. As don Juan says, "For a warrior there can be no greater love" (IV-285).

THE SOLITUDE OF A WARRIOR

Paradoxically, warriors also know what it means to be alone since they are aware that their struggle is strictly their responsibility, each life a personal journey. But the solitude of warriors is of a nature very distinct from the solitude of loneliness experienced by an average person. It is not painful or full of need. It is experienced as a joyful secret that permits them to intensely love everything that they touch, look at, or feel—they know how quickly life passes and have learned how to love from the inexhaustible and disinterested love emanating from the Earth. With devotion to the Earth as the fundamental feeling, they establish an intimate and warm relationship with nature and with people.

Thus warriors express in their person that peculiar equilibrium between two poles of an apparently irresolvable contradiction: they are solitary beings who are never alone. Immersed in this contradiction, they are aware of aloneness, knowing that being alone is nothing more than a human concern having to do only with the tonal. They know—having been there—that there exists a reality beyond the apparent one, in which a human being is but a piece of light hardly differentiated, and only for a brief instant, against the great fountain that is our origin and destiny—the Earth.

THE ANTIDOTE FOR LONELINESS

If you were to ask for an antidote to the anguish of human loneliness, I would suggest that you reencounter and reexamine the connection that unites us with the Earth, our lost "umbilical cord." I would invite you to recognize the presence of an inexhaustible love that remains unaffected by human affairs. It is not so difficult. Look around, remember the being that sustains us, and realize you are at home, always at home.

I believe that in schools, before they learn to add and subtract, to buy and sell, to fear and lie, our children should learn to love and respect the being that gives them refuge. I have had the good fortune to see how the lives of people change and are enriched by simply opening their eyes to accept and return the embrace of the Earth; they learn that each being of nature is kindred, born of the same womb. In these moments our everyday attachments—such as anger, competition, envy, possessiveness, hungers, and unsatisfied needs—seem insignificant alongside more noble presences. Our limited world is suddenly transformed into a much larger world made beautiful by the many beings it contains. Trees become significant; birds, whales, flowers, dogs, humans, rivers, and mountains all become what they really are—our natural heritage to be enjoyed and loved but not possessed. We accept the personal privilege of witnessing its presence, if only for the short duration of our existence as mortals. Allowing ourselves to be affected by the beauty and the mystery of nature in all her expressions is to accept the gift of the Earth and to recognize our forgotten nature. We are also beings in this world, another detail of the scenery. The same magic and mystery beats and moves within each one of us. We then, without reserve, occupy the place that belongs to us within the great concert of nature.

TECHNIQUES

An infinite number of practices can serve to reconnect us with nature and with the Earth. Anything will do: taking a walk, climbing a mountain, swimming a river, petting a dog, or hugging a human being, as long as our attention is focused on the encounter itself and not on its usefulness. We should visit natural environments often—taking great care to avoid damaging them—with our heart and attention wide open to listen to nature's message, to reencounter also our own natural being. We should get away from the cities where human affairs destroy everything, and enter as often as possible into the world where everything occurs as it should. If we are attentive and perceptive, we can learn the rhythm of nature, the very rhythm we lack in our own lives. Many people have asked me about masters. I personally know of no master more knowledgeable than nature. It is quite enough to observe and imitate her.

My work groups—climbing snow-covered peaks, rafting through turbulent rapids, taking long hikes across the desert or through tropical jungle, and penetrating into the Earth through grottos and caverns—find that direct encounters with nature within a context of effort and learning are extraordinarily enriching. Sports in the open air, those mentioned and many others, can serve as a doorway to reestablish contact with the Earth and optimize the use of personal energy, especially if those efforts are combined with the nonordinary uses of attention as described throughout this book.

By way of example, here are some of the unusual procedures that have given beautiful and surprising results in reconnecting us with the awareness of the Earth.

73. ALPINISM ARBOREAL

This technique has to do with an activity that many of us knew as children and that we did only for fun—climbing trees. In this case, however, we will be dealing with something a little more elaborate.

My interest in trees arises from a personal experience upon encountering something much acknowledged in many ancient indigenous traditions, including don Juan's—the natural empathy that trees have for human beings. On many occasions I have been able to prove this affinity. In each, one or several trees have helped in several ways: relieving sadness, revealing some secret, curing a nonphysical illness, filling the spirit with peace, or simply teaching a song. Even the average person can verify that trees are extraordinarily splendid beings in their relationship with humans. They treat us to their scenic beauty, they transmit to us tranquillity and harmony when we look at them, they provide for rest in their shade, they give shelter and comfort with their wood, and they provide oxygen to breathe. While we insist on contaminating the atmosphere, they go to great lengths to clean it. And there is much more within the awareness of trees, if we are capable of opening ourselves to it.

The exercise consists of climbing a tree and—once situated—practicing not-doings to allow you to link yourself with the awareness of the tree. Any tree will do as long as its trunk and branches are strong enough to support your weight without fear of breakage. Also your approach to the tree should be open and respectful. You must be extremely careful not to injure the tree in any way if you hope to establish a good relationship with it.

To begin, first contemplate the tree awhile before climbing it, letting feelings of sympathy flow toward it, as it will no doubt notice. Next, talk to it—convey greetings and ask permission to climb it, explaining your motive for doing so and assuring it that you will be very careful. Merely talking aloud to a tree can be an immense help for dispelling confusion or sadness in moments when you need advice.

When you are ready to climb, choose a tree of moderate height that has branches close to the ground to facilitate ascent. To climb, use the "three point technique," making sure three extremities are well supported while moving the fourth. For example, stand with both feet on a limb with the right hand firmly grasping a branch before moving the left hand to a new point of support. Or lift the right leg to a higher branch while maintaining both hands and the left foot on a firm support. Should the point you are reaching for give way, you won't fall since three points of support will keep you firmly supported. Just remember: move one extremity at a time while keeping the others securely anchored.

Branches are stronger and more resistant to weight at the point where they join the trunk, so step as close to the trunk as possible, especially when thinner branches are involved.

As you gain experience, this exercise can take on a character more like mountain climbing—tackling trees as high as 100 feet, reaching the lowest limbs even several yards above the ground. Small branch stumps, knots, and hollows in the bark can serve as points of support for the experienced tree climber. In work groups, we often joke that a tree has not truly been climbed until our navel projects above the crown of the tree, while we are balanced on its topmost branches. It is less difficult than it seems, but it is necessary to learn little by little so as not to injure yourself or the trees. We have specialized in climbing conifers like ones found in woods in Michoacan, Puebla, and the state of Mexico[18], but almost any type of tree would work as well.

---

[18] These refer to areas of the Mexican republic.

Climbing a tree while maintaining alertness and concentration constitutes the basic exercise. The higher and more complicated the climb, the better. Once at the top many exercises can be performed; for example:

- Find a place to rest among the high branches, learning to adjust body posture to their configuration.

- Practice "merging" your awareness with that of the tree, visualizing yourself as another branch of the tree, trying to assimilate its state of being, feeling and rocking with the wind.

- Observe the tree taking note of the feelings that it produces in you. Form them into a song.

- Spend the night in a tree. If you are not experienced at this, tie yourself to reduce the risk of falling while asleep. A variation, which can be used for purposes of purification, is to hang a hammock between two high branches and spend the night there. An appropriate precaution against falling is to lace the edges of the hammock shut in such a way that you are totally enclosed.

- Tell the tree your sorrows or what makes you happy, according to the circumstances.

Make up your own exercises or learn some directly from the trees themselves, which, not for nothing, are called our big brothers.

74. THE RHYTHM OF THE EARTH

This exercise is at once very easy and very difficult—although the procedure is very simple, it requires a special state of being to carry out. We must be capable—by our own means—of reaching a state of heightened attention in order to involve ourselves in the task without reserve or anxiety. Of course, a certain amount of available energy is required as well. I mention the procedure here, having already established that this experience is well within the reach of almost all who have worked continuously and sincerely in saving energy, in cultivating attention, and in integrating themselves with nature.

The exercise consists of taking a hike, which can include alternately walking, jogging, or running. One fundamental aspect of this exercise is finding and maintaining the same rhythm in your pace as well as in your breathing; they must remain synchronized. For this to be fully carried out, your rhythm must be assimilated from the rhythm of the Earth. Only the Earth can teach you her own rhythm; your task is to achieve the connection.

There is not much to say regarding a procedure for achieving this. I can make a suggestion from my own experience: look for this connection by taking a long hike through the mountains, the jungle, or the desert in an uninhabited zone, away from highways and populated areas. (With my groups in Mexico, we sometimes hike through a portion of the Sierra Norte in the state of Puebla.)

The hike should last several days, with the objective of simply walking and training the attention. Begin by walking in the manner described in the walk of attention (exercise 34). Concentrate on finding and maintaining a rhythm between walking and breathing; this should not be altered for irregularities in the terrain, such as in ascents and descents. Keep walking until you have achieved connection with the Earth, changing to a jog only if the body is motivated spontaneously to do so without intervention of mind or desire. The same applies to running. It is possible to combine them, changing from a walk to a jog, and a jog to a run, according to the configuration of the terrain or bodily feeling. The trick is to maintain the same rhythm in spite of any change in velocity.

Do not forget the Earth at any moment; remain aware that you are walking on her. You can convert each step into a remembrance of the Earth, caressing her with the feet without letting this affect in any way the natural way of walking. The longer you walk without interruption, the greater will be your chances for success, since the sharpening of the attention is one of the principal ingredients for achieving this link with the Earth's awareness. When this occurs, you are no longer the walker moving yourself along. Rather you are propelled by a force—what is known as the Earth's boost (VII-222)—which can change your walk into an all-out run whose velocity can surpass all expectations. Needless to say, when this occurs, fatigue, time, and distance are parameters that no longer function. There is no room for speculation when this connection is made since the feeling of being possessed by a power beyond the self is so overwhelming.

75. THE BURIAL OF THE WARRIOR

Carlos Castaneda makes reference in different parts of his work (III-121–123), (VI-11–12) to the practice of warriors burying themselves. He says that warriors bury themselves in the Earth to find clarity or to receive instructions or to cure themselves of a malady. However, he does not go into great detail.

I have experienced voluntary burial and I have assisted others in achieving it as well. In these experiences, I have witnessed some of the many and varied effects—all beneficial—it has on the practitioner. A few examples:

- Recapitulation is enhanced while we are buried, due to the enormous force of the Earth, who knows of our task and collaborates with us.

- When people who have experienced very painful losses or who are in states of depression are buried, the Earth has shown that she can heal emotional wounds better than anyone since she has the capacity to absorb all types of unpleasantness.

- The Earth can help us to find answers and clarity in personal matters.

- The Earth can help to recharge our energy before or after a particularly demanding task or challenge.

- The Earth can help us penetrate into aspects of the other self.

- At the point of experiencing significant change in our lives, we can bury our old self and allow the birth of our new being.

When we bury ourselves, we can obtain help from the Earth for just about anything as long as we have a clear purpose. The more clear our purpose, the more clear and conclusive will be the result.

I have practiced two types of burial: above ground (by constructing a "cage of earth") and below ground. The types can be used interchangeably, although I personally consider below ground better when there is great urgency.

Normally—above all the first few times—the assistance of another person will be required, preferably someone who has experienced this exercise himself or herself. The assistant's fundamental role will be to watch over you while you are buried, keeping outside disturbances away and offering any kind of help needed. Generally, when you are buried for the first time, you will enter more freely into the exercise if you know someone you trust is "caring" for you. The instructions are:

1. Select an appropriate spot for burial. It must be in an uninhabited area, preferably among trees. Beginners should avoid the desert, the jungle, and near the ocean or large rivers. Also avoid areas where spectators are likely to disturb you or be alarmed by your activities. Avoid anthills, insect nests, and snakes. Places with a high energy content are appropriate if you are familiar with such places. Under no circumstances should this exercise be done near archaeological ruins or a cemetery. A simple forest will be quite appropriate.

2. Find a specific site within the chosen area, trying to "sense with the eyes" (III-66) a place that appeals to you in some way. Avoid slopes or the edges of gorges and ravines, as well as damp areas.

3. With a stick, mark off the area required to bury yourself lying down—rectangular in shape, a little longer and

wider than the body, just large enough to lie in with a blanket in case you will be staying for any length of time and it happens to be cold. The "tomb" should be oriented so your head points toward your favorable direction[19]. If that is not known, choose the east or the south.

4. Now begin digging a tomb in the Earth, using some kind of pointed stick. Depth should be a little less than two feet. The excavated soil should be piled next to the tomb on the left side.

5. Next gather enough fairly straight sticks around 2½ feet long to make a covering for the tomb and branches with foliage and large leaves to seal the spaces between the sticks to prevent dirt from falling through when the tomb is covered with soil. The sticks, branches, and leaves, should be piled next to the tomb to be on hand as needed.

6. Begin closing the grave by placing the sticks crossways very close together, starting from the feet end and going up to the shoulders. Place the leaves and branches over the sticks and—finally—place soil over these until the sticks and branches are totally covered. Some kind of cotton cloth or other nonsynthetic fabric the size of the body may be placed between the sticks and the branches to prevent dirt from filtering through.

7. Now prepare for entry into the tomb. It is best to have an almost empty stomach and to relieve yourself beforehand. Drinking a little water is also a good idea. As a preparation, you can perform some of the exercises of the skeleton (exercises 19, 20, 21) mentioned in the section on the awareness of death. Or a personal ritual dealing with your departure from the world can be performed if you are practicing this exercise for purposes of change.

8. Enter the tomb feet first through the hole left at shoulder height being careful not to disturb the sticks or the soil upon entering.

9. Once inside, complete the covering of the tomb by carefully placing the rest of the sticks, branches, leaves, and

---

[19] You must find for yourself the most appropriate method to find the true direction.

soil. You can do this from inside the tomb, or the assistant can close up the tomb from the outside. In any case, make sure to leave a small hole (4" by 4") to allow entry of air (but not of light should this exercise be done during the day). One way to deal with the problem of light is to locate the air hole near the feet, with the head end completely sealed.

10. Submerge yourself in the experience until it is time to come out.

Here are some additional considerations:

• Each step should be considered part of a ritual in which the digging, gathering branches and covering with soil are all done without talking or any other kind of dispersal of attention. This is done so that when you bury yourself, you will have achieved a sharper state of awareness through attention.

• The ideal way to do this exercise is in the nude—especially when it is used for the treatment of ill health or serious illnesses of the spirit—in which case cold climates must be avoided. Take into account that below ground temperature is colder than atmospheric temperature and that soil tends to retain dampness. If it must be done at low temperatures, you should be dressed and take along a blanket or sleeping bag. You may also use a small pillow.

• Do not allow yourself to be frightened by what might occur while buried. Many things considered unusual in the everyday world are normal during burial—voices, visions, experiences beyond the confines of the tomb itself, feelings, or revelations. The burial of the warrior is a voyage, but in any case, you can be sure it will be a trip to there and back again. Maintain sobriety and face whatever is necessary. Attention to breathing and singing songs of power (or creating some on the spur of the moment) can help maintain sobriety.

• Let feelings flow freely through laughter, crying, songs, words, moods, or whatever the body requires.

• The period of burial can vary a great deal according to the warrior and the circumstances of burial. Remaining buried all one night or all one day is usually enough. With a little practice or in cases of necessity, you can remain for 24 hours or more. For periods of more than 24 hours you should be buried with some light nutritious snacks such as dried fruit, and cereal, and water. Combining burial with the practice of fasting should be done only under the strict supervision of someone who has experience in these matters.

• The best hour for terminating the exercise and leaving the tomb is in the predawn twilight, or occasionally during sunset.

For burial above ground using the cage-of-earth method, follow the same steps outlined above, but instead of digging a hole in the ground, gather sticks, roughly two feet in length that form a "Y" shape on the upper end, to be used as supports for the transverse sticks. The other end is inserted into the ground. Once "the cage" is constructed, it is covered with branches and leaves and then with soil. During construction, the head end is left open to facilitate entry when the moment arrives.

76. A REENCOUNTER WITH THE EARTH

This exercise can serve as either a prelude or a finale to the other exercises detailed in this section. It deals with the intimate experience of a reencounter with the Earth, like the reunion of two beings who love each other but haven't seen each other for a long time.

For this reunion, choose a place that no one else knows about—a place that can remain a secret forever. You may know of a place beforehand, or you can go out and look for one. Preferably it should be in a remote location. If reaching it requires a long walk or climb, so much the better. However, in reality any place chosen for an appointment with the Earth will do since there is no way she will slight you by not responding to your encounter.

Arriving at your place, lie face down on the Earth, embracing her. You must feel and soak yourself in her presence. Then—still embracing and caressing her—begin to talk aloud to her, using intimate and personal words, telling her how grateful you are that she responded to your call, and for always having been there. Explain to her the world from which you have come and why you had forgotten her. Tell her of those lonely moments of life when you did not remember her, of the lack you felt, and how happy this reencounter makes you. Offer her one or two actions that you will carry out in the daily world that will help you remain aware of her presence and company. And finally, promise not to forget her again but to love her until the moment arrives when she again takes you into her bosom to free you from all burdens.

At last, give her a kiss and return to the world, immersed in her secret and loving embrace . . .

ADDITIONAL
CONSIDERATIONS

To finish up this present volume, I would like to add some considerations relating to the material presented throughout the preceding pages. What has been presented represents one of the fundamental pillars of my work as investigator and coordinator of work groups. It does not encompass all of its aspects.

For twelve years I have worked simultaneously with groups and in field investigations using a new form of anthropology that I term anti-anthropology, offering new possibilities in the fields of psychology and psychotherapy, nourished by the encounter with nature and what I would dare call Toltec psychology. Anti-anthropology regards human beings from the point of view of wholeness far more than what we know in modern societies.

The work in groups has served as a testing ground for applying the results gleaned from field investigations, and in its turn has been one more aspect of the investigation itself. Thus, field work outside the groups has nourished the functional development of group work, and this development has contributed new elements that have nourished the investigation in the field, as well as the group work itself.

The themes, objectives, and theoretical frameworks, of my investigations prove too complex, extensive, and above all inappropriate, to try to explain at this time. This is not a work of theory or methodology but of concrete practice. It is directed not toward theoretical or special investigators but toward the restless individual who desires to explore new possibilities of experience, knowledge, and freedom to the point where he or she is responsible enough for personal experimenting, in place of being content only with thinking, imagining, or conversing.

The fundamental theme of these investigations and my work in general is, naturally, human beings and their unexplored possibilities. My restlessness as an investigator has not been much different from the natural restlessness of any human being, especially the ones who have discovered their own mortal questions: Who are we? Of what are we made? Why am I not happy? Do I have to live exactly like everyone else? Can I choose? Is there an alternative? Are there other realities?

In the encounter with the "otherness", I have discovered that there *are* alternatives and that another way to live does exist. We truly can choose and make for ourselves a world and a life that exists in harmony with the aspirations of our spirit. I am not saying this is easy. I am saying it is possible. I can say it because I have proven it to myself. The truth is that achieving it requires us to detach ourselves from many of the habitual conceptions that we have assimilated from our society and to recover parts of our being that society has encouraged us to forget altogether. As don Juan said, inside all of us there is hidden a sorcerer (VII-210) for whom we secretly yearn. We yearn for the magic, the mystery, and the freedom of that sorcerer.

My curiosity to know about human beings and their possibilities is what brought me to the study of anthropology; the encounter with indigenous peoples is what caused me to adopt anti-anthropology with the aim of transforming myself instead of transforming them. From them I also learned that while psychology and psychoanalysis hold a limited view of the human being based on our Western way of life, the indigenous cosmovision reveals facets of awareness unexplored by modern science. From these we could develop forms of therapy (sometimes called ethnotherapy) based on the knowledge these indigenous cultures possess about human nature.

My encounters with nature in her many forms—particularly with the mountains, the trees, and marine mammals—allowed me to discover that nature herself was the best therapist and teacher I could find.

Over the years I found that I had put together a great quantity of material and experience that was reflected in the consistent results made manifest through the efforts of those participating in the groups. It seemed this material could make novel contributions to the human sciences in general and to anthropology, psychology, and psychotherapy, in particular. Restless young people, innovators, and specialists in these areas participated in the work in order to enrich their own. The requirements of these specialists and the certainty that the results of this work could have benefits for the work of others—as the work of others at times enriched mine—brought me to the conclusion that I had to put these discoveries down in writing.

The accumulation of information, facts, and experience—in a certain way so diverse—was such that it demanded not one but several works encompassing the principal areas of this work.

I decided that the first to be published would be that which related to the work of Carlos Castaneda. The task of practical application of the proposals contained in his books—together with my experiences among the Indians—has constituted one of the central axes of my work. And I hope to establish a first point of contact with those many people who, though also restless, would nevertheless remain ignorant of these experiences. The material presented here does not include all of the practices that have been developed. Rather it deals mainly with the fundamentals of those exercises that can be practiced without the need of a guide or a work group, strictly to aid the work of the "solitary warrior".

There are three other works in progress. The first will be a treatise on the applicability of my discoveries in the practice of anthropology, psychology, and psychotherapy. The second will be on my experience and methods of work in the formation of encounter groups and their development. A third book will deal with poetic experiences (in the widest sense of the term) that have been shared in the work groups. In this last one I hope to relate not only moments of amazing magic but also some of the many stories, poems, and songs that have risen up in the heat of group encounters.

Besides these, I have material in restricted circulation, directed toward specialists interested in the formation and coordination of groups.

If you desire more information about any aspect of this work, make contact through courses, seminars, and workshops that are offered from time to time, or write to the following address:

Victor Sánchez
Apartado Postal No. 12-762
C.P.03001
Mexico, D.F.
Mexico

BIBLIOGRAPHY OF BOOKS
BY CARLOS CASTANEDA

(I) *The Teachings of Don Juan,*
Simon and Schuster,
Pocket Books, 1974, New York, N.Y.

(II) *A Separate Reality,*
Penguin Books Ltd, 1973,
Harmondsworth, Middlesex, England

(III) *Journey to Ixtlan,*
Penguin Books Ltd, 1974,
Harmondsworth, Middlesex, England

(IV) *Tales of Power,*
Simon and Schuster, 1974, New York, N.Y.

(V) *The Second Ring of Power,*
Simon and Schuster, Touchstone edition,
1979, New York, N.Y.

(VI) *The Eagle's Gift,*
Simon and Schuster,
Pocket Books, 1982, New York, N.Y.

(VII) *The Fire From Within,*
Transworld Publishers,
Black Swan edition, 1984, London

(VIII) *The Power of Silence,*
Simon and Schuster, 1987, New York, N.Y.

GLOSSARY OF TECHNIQUES FROM THE WORKS OF CARLOS CASTANEDA

1 CORPORAL PERCEPTION
   Power spot I-29–34
   Power spot II-235–236
   Power spot III-66, 162
   Power spot and leaves for the umbilical region III-176–179
   Bed of strings III-162
   Sniffing III-129
   Massage for perceiving with the calves VI-255
   Mid-point VII-125

2 WALKS OF ATTENTION AND THE GAIT OF POWER
   A form of walking III-35
   Following the footprints III-157
   Gait of power III-183
   Walking and the internal dialogue IV-21
   Right way of walking IV-232
   Walking with the arms behind V-251–252
   Gait of power VII-148

3 STOPPING THE INTERNAL DIALOGUE
   Attention (see number 4)
   Listening II-225
   Holes between the sounds II-228, 230, 232
   Looking at shadows III-213
   A form of walking III-35
   Internal dialogue and walking IV-21
   Unfocused vision V-295
   Dreaming and the internal dialogue VI-135–137
   Women and the internal dialogue VI-136

4 ATTENTION

Not-doing (see number 5)
Walks and gaits (see number 2)
Stopping the internal dialogue (see number 3)
Spirit catcher II-233
Looking at the fog III-141
Attention and sound III-144
Observing shadows III-194
Observing a piece of cloth III-200
Observing a rock III-203
Shadows and crossing the eyes III-210
Looking through half-closed eyes III-216
Finding a place with allies III-220
Call of moths V-147
A way of eating V-222–223
Observing hills, clouds, etc. V-240
Gazing for second attention and dreaming V-284–289
Gazing at a piece of cloth V-293–297
Harness game VI-61–62
Purifying harness VI-184
Feeling the assemblage point VI-252–253
Cotton bag VI-255
Harness VI-262, 302
Pelvic movement. Assemblage point and dreaming
    VII-292–293
Calling intent VII-283

5 NOT-DOING

Attention (see number 4)
Hat with mirrors VI-137
Box of not-doing VI-234
Changing levels of awareness VI-235
Separating hearing from sight VI-235
Suspended in a tree VI-235–236

6 NOT-DOINGS OF THE PERSONAL SELF

Death as an adviser III-43
Death as an adviser IV-236
Erasing personal history III-26
Disrupting routines III-89

Telling lies III-213
Changing facades IV-236
Losing self-importance III-35
Talking to plants III-40
Acting for the sake of acting IV-232–233
Caring for another VI-130
Assuming responsibility III-53
Gesture III-60

7 STALKING
Not doings of the personal self (see number 6)
Becoming a hunter III-64
Being inaccessible III-75
Observing tonals IV-137
Stalking habits V-222
Equanimity in social situations VI-134
Principles of stalking VI-278–281, 291
Precepts of stalking VI-279
Recapitulation VI-284–289
Elements of strategy VII-31
Petty tyrant VII-31–34, 38, 39, 46
Habits and the assemblage point VII-136–138
Stalking and the assemblage point VII-187–188
Acting deliberately VII-196
Disguises VIII-84–85
Disguised as the opposite sex VIII-87–88
Poems and inner silence VIII-130–131
Intending appearances VIII-280–282
The four moods of stalking VII-88–106

8 DREAMING
Not-doing (see number 5)
Setting up dreaming III-114
Dreaming III-127–128
Head band III-147
Dreaming III-167–168, 173–174
Dreaming IV-20
Dreaming V-159
Holding dream images V-268
Dreaming V-268–269

GLOSSARY OF TECHNIQUES FROM THIS BOOK

THE BODY AS A FIELD OF ENERGY

1. Inventory of energy expenditures
2. Technique for determining the energetic quality of your acts
3. References for determining your energy level at birth
4. Technique for stopping emotions or debilitating thoughts
5 Technique for saving energy and well-being
6. Technique of silence
7. Saving sexual energy
8. Capturing energy from the Sun

THE ART OF STALKING AND ITS PRACTICE

Recapitulation

9. The list of events
10. Breathing
11. The recapitulation box

Other Exercises

12. The stalker's strategy
13. Intending appearances
14. Actor for a few days
15. Disguises
16. Disguised as a member of the opposite sex
17. Observing tonals

THE NOT-DOINGS OF THE PERSONAL SELF

The Awareness of Death

18. Death as an adviser

The Awareness of the Skeleton

19. Awakening the skeleton
20. Touching the skeleton
21. The dance of the skeleton

50. The candle of silence
51. Arts and sports

THE MAGIC OF ATTENTION

52. Observing shadows
53. Observing rocks
54. The tree made of sky
55. Walking backward
56. The hat with mirror
57. Suspended from the ceiling
58. Suspended from a tree

SETTING UP DREAMING

59. Finding your hands
60. Sustaining dream images
61. Learning to move
62. Space and time
63. Finding yourself
64. Some suggestions of a technical nature
65. The observation of *dreaming* objects

THE BODY AS AWARENESS

Corporal Perception
66. The walk of the midpoint
67. The bed of strings

Exercises Without Seeing
68. Exercise of the blind
69. The home of the blind
70. The walk of the blind
71. The call
72. Race to the unknown

THE WARRIOR'S GREATEST LOVE

Relating to the Earth and to Nature
73. Alpinism arboreal
74. The rhythm of the Earth
75. The burial of the warrior
76. A reencounter with the Earth

ANNOTATED TABLE
OF CONTENTS

Chapter 4
The Art of Stalking and its Practice

PART THREE: THE ACCESS TO THE SEPARATE REALITY
(Practices for the Left Side)

Chapter 6
Stopping the Internal Dialogue or the Key to the Door between
the Worlds